Paperclay
Art and practice

Paperclay
Art and practice

Rosette Gault

University of Pennsylvania Press • Philadelphia

Bloomsbury Visual Arts
An imprint of Bloomsbury Publishing Plc

BLOOMSBURY
LONDON • NEW DELHI • NEW YORK • SYDNEY

Bloomsbury Visual Arts
An imprint of Bloomsbury Publishing Plc
Imprint previously known as A&C Black Visual Arts

50 Bedford Square   1385 Broadway
London   New York
WC1B 3DP   NY 10018
UK   USA

www.bloomsbury.com
BLOOMSBURY and the Diana logo are trademarks of Bloomsbury
Publishing Plc

First published in 2013
Reprinted in 2014

Published simultaneously in the U.S.A by
University of Pennsylvania Press
3905 Spruce Street
Philadelphia, PA 19104-4112
www.pennpress.org

© Rosette Gault 2013

British Library Cataloguing-in-Publication Data
A catalogue record for this book is available from the British Library
and the US Library of Congress.

ISBN PB: 978-1-4081-3120-6
US ed: 978-0-8122-2241-8

Typeset in 10 on 13pt Rotis Semi Sans
Book design by Susan McIntyre
Cover design by Sutchinda Thompson
Printed and bound in China.

Dedication
To the spirit of art in the world.

Acknowledgements
Research for this big project was sponsored in part by a series
of artist residency grants from the Banff Centre for the Arts in
Alberta, Canada, the International Ceramic Research Center at
Guldagergaard, Denmark, the Bechyne
Ceramic Symposium of the Czech Republic, the International
Ceramics Studio in Kesckemét, Hungary, and New Century
Arts, Inc., USA.

Besides my editor Kate Sherington, I also thank Alison
Stace for her extra work on earlier versions. Gayle St Luise,
with the support of her husband Greg Funk, devoted
countless extra hours to this book.

In addition to hundreds of contributors to the book,
from every continent, acknowledged throughout and on my
website at www.paperclayart.com/191ThankYou.html, there
are thousands more behind the scenes to be thanked, who
have lent many forms of support over the 40-plus years I have
been researching this subject. As Ira Progoff might say: "This
was solitary work I could never have done alone." Some of the
most talented and imaginative artists have been involved.

front cover: Barbro Åberg (Denmark), *Momentum*, 2007.
Paperclay with perlite, 67 x 44 x 25 cm (17¼ x 26½ x 9¾ in.).
Photo: Lars Henrik Mardahl; Derek Au (China), celadon
dinner set. Porcelain paperclay. *Photo: courtesy of Derek Au.*
back cover: Angela Mellor (UK), *Ocean Light* bowl, 1997. Bone
china with paperclay slip inlay, 12 x 18.5 cm (4¾ x 7¼ in.).
Photo: Victor France; Ingrid Bathe (USA), *Star platter*, 2011.
Porcelain paperclay, 35.5 x 35.5 x 6.5 cm (14 x 14 x 2½ in.).
Photo: courtesy of the artist; Barbro Åberg (Denmark),
Double Spiral Wheel, 2009. Paperclay with perlite, 44 x 44 x
8 cm (17¼ x 17¼ x 3 in.). *Photo: Lars Henrik Mardahl.*
frontispiece: Nuala O'Donavan (Ireland), *Teasel, Three Sided,*
2010. *Photo: Sylvain Deleu.*
contents page: Einat Cohen (Israel), *Shells*, 2009. Porcelain
paperclay, hand-built, clear glaze, diameter: 55 cm (21½ in.).
Photo: Einat Cohen.

Contents

Introduction

In the artist's hand, the dynamic modelling medium known as 'paperclay' becomes an instrument of awareness, a vehicle for imagination and memory, a record of human touch and, often, a connection to the spirit of beauty and wonder. It is a practical means by which an artist's vision can be realised and thus shared with the world. In this book, we will see ways that a language of universal imagination called visual art can cross boundaries and link collective and personal visions that might otherwise be invisible. In addition, many of the works in the book are technically impossible to build in traditional clay, and as such, offer tangible evidence of a highly contagious yearning for expressive freedom that communicates across divides in time, space and culture.

This book will highlight aesthetic and technical advances, contributions and explorations that have occurred in the field of paperclay over the last 20 years. In addition to practical content, the book showcases a small sample of works from artists practicing in every continent of the world.

Irit Abba (Israel), collection of vases, 2009. Wheel-thrown and hand-built with stained porcelain paperclay, height: 71 cm (28 in.). *Photo: Ohad Matalon.*

ABOVE LEFT: Carmen Lang (USA/Mexico), *Pool*, 2010. Stoneware paperclay, 12.5 x 38 cm (5 x 15 in.). *Photo: Carmen Lang.*

ABOVE RIGHT: Eszter Imre (Sweden/Hungary), *Poetry: It is about …*, 2011. Porcelain paperclay, 20 x 15 cm (8 x 6 in.). *Photo: Mats Ringquist.*

Although the medium shares some properties with traditional pottery clays, it also has distinct properties that allow alternative working methods, extending the reach of an artist's imagination beyond many of the technical limitations of traditional clay. New rules or principles specific to paperclay art and practice can now be more clearly seen. A high proportion of traditional beliefs and assumptions about ceramic practice have at the least been called into question and some have been overturned completely. Furthermore, a non-linear approach to creation with paperclay allows visions to emerge that we have never seen before.

Close to 300 artists from 38 countries contributed to this book, so in reading it you will see a global view of the wide range of ideas that artists are exploring with paperclay, as well as, I hope, a vicarious sense of the hands-on creative process, even if you are new to hands-on clay practice of any kind. It is also informed by my 40 years of ceramic art practice and research. What you will find here is testimony to the creativity of those who, as a group, opened the way to a flowering of fresh perspective, vision and enthusiasm. The spirit of expanded expressive freedom and discovery behind it all has had added a significant dimension to the field of contemporary ceramics.

Rosette Gault, May 2012

Meet paperclay

About paperclay

Paperclay ceramic, as an artist's medium, is a water-based compound of clay minerals and cellulose fibre that hardens in the open air and/or can be fired and glazed in kilns. Hidden inside the paperclay is a flexible three-dimensional network or lattice of water-absorbent cellulose fibres. The fibres come from either virgin or recycled paper pulps (derived from cotton, linen, flax, hemp or wood), and both inks and fibres burn away in the kiln. Paperclay ceramic contains enough clay that it can be glazed and fired like traditional clay. After firing, the exterior look and feel of paperclay is, in essence, indistinguishable from the traditional ceramic, except that the paperclay ceramic might weigh less. The fired result can be watertight or porous as desired.

As a building material, it is dynamic and versatile. It is strong and pliant to model with, and can be modelled and assembled in all its moisture states, including dry and fired. Depending on their requirements, artists today can use fired or non-fired paperclay, alone or in combination. Whether gloss or matt, durable paperclay ceramic finishes can mimic almost every known sculpture or building material (see p. 154). Commercial modelling compounds, air-hardening clay and pâpier maché share some but not all of its properties.

LEFT: Malia Landis (USA), *Pueo Nesting in the Gardenia*, 2008. Paperclay, 40.5 x 30.5 x 20 cm (16 x 12 x 8 in.). *Photo: Malia Landis.*

RIGHT: Ingrid Bathe (USA), *Salt and Pepper*, 2012. Porcelain paperclay, 4 x 18 x 7.5 cm (1½ x 7 x 3 in.). *Photo: Ingrid Bathe.*

Handling paperclay

Familiar methods of pinch, coil, slab and wheel-throwing carry over to paperclay. At the leathersoft stage, it feels and handles similarly to traditional clay to press, roll, stretch, or to stamp impressions or textures in. Because of the fibre, soft coils can feel more like string or rope, and when rolled out will usually reach a longer length than traditional clay, too. At the leathersoft stage, it can feel strong like wet fabric or flexible like poster board. It can be left to dry and harden in the open air, or even be force-dried if desired.

In the form of a watered-down slurry or paste, paperclay slip can be an adhesive, a coating or a casting medium. It is a popular patch, crack and gap filler for dry and some types of fired cracks.

Dry or 'green' (unfired) forms of paperclay feel harder and denser than most cardboard, but a bit softer than wood and drywall. Dry paperclay is tough enough to be transported safely. To compare, when paperclay is bone-dry or 'cured', the tensile strength before firing can be nearly double that of a non-paperclay body (see p. 151). Dry or bisque forms of paperclay are strong enough to be worked with hammer, chisel, drills, saws and lasers, can serve for simple press moulds, or can be used to imprint and stamp soft clay.

Infinite changes to the form of dry-state paperclay are possible. These include freedom to assemble, join, cut, paste, repair, add, subtract and carve, with as many wet-dry-wet episodes as are needed or desired. A dry paperclay form is stable through all this. In a manner similar to wood, the paperclay form expands, contracts and pauses in its movement according to its moisture content.

Switch between dry and wet-state paperclay to your heart's content before the piece is completed. It is possible to recombine or replace parts – such as handles, ears, tails and so forth – at almost any time in the course of construction.

Bisque firing is optional; single firing is feasible because the dry ware is strong and absorbent enough to be glazed without deforming. When a kiln firing is not planned, air-set or cold finishes will serve. Thin areas of dry paperclay eventually re-soften in moisture.

ABOVE LEFT: The feel of paperclay: pinch open a small bowl in soft clay to get a sense of how much pressure is needed. Soft paperclay gradually starts to stiffen and harden in air. *Photo: Rosette Gault.*

ABOVE RIGHT: Replace a broken coil tip by placing a fresh soft coil extension onto the dry part. Dip the dry end in water, apply a dab or two of paperclay slip, press the soft part on and smooth the join. The glass bowl acts as a temporary support. *Photo: Rosette Gault.*

Compared to what you might be used to, paperclay has a new feel. Your skill level and goals will determine whether a sculptor's (high pulp) or potter's (low pulp) mix feels better.
Photo: Rosette Gault.

Sam Davies (Australia), a complex braided coil, work in progress, 2010. The cultural influence of Australian Aboriginal textile and weaving traditions is visible in this work.
Photo: Sam Davies.

In brief: how it's mixed, how it's made

Typically, a measure of wet cellulose fibre pulp, sourced from recycled paper, is stirred into a smooth clay base. The result will be a ready-to-use oatmeal-looking slurry, or *paperclay slip*, which can be used as an all-purpose pouring, adhesive or dipping mix. As the water evaporates, the slip thickens to a soft paste. In due course, the mix stiffens to a soft clay modelling consistency.

To recycle newsprint paper, for example, small pieces are soaked in a soup of water until the fibres soften. Then the mix is agitated until the entangled fibres loosen and are floating freely in the water. This wet pulp is gathered up from the water in a sieve or mesh bag and stirred into a clay slip.

Jeoung-Ah Kim (Korea/ Sweden), *Tableware*, 2004. Slip-cast porcelain paperclay, fired to 1360°C (2480°F), with gold ceramic lustre. *Photo: Jeoung-Ah Kim.*

Many artists prefer to create quality, custom blends in small quantities in the studio. Detailed instruction on how to prepare these are described in the next chapter. Some prefer commercial ready-blends of prepared paperclays. Contact information for suppliers is provided at the back of this book (p. 157). Ceramic paperclays as described in this book are sometimes referred to as fibre clay, flax clay, P'Clay®, P'Slip® and paperslip.

Approaches to making with paperclay

Two approaches

Paperclay is popular to work with because it can be approached in so many ways. The initial process of modelling paperclay forms is almost the same as traditional clay. But what happens next? At this point, you can choose between two working processes. If you follow the familiar and traditional approach, your work will continue in a one way or 'linear' sequence of forming, assembly and finishing until complete. If you try a non-linear approach, the end result will come about by practices that would be impractical or impossible in traditional clay. For example, a non-linear approach allows you to re-wet a section of dry paperclay and make changes or repairs to it. Ceramic artists who have grown frustrated or felt limited by traditional methods needed for working clay now have an alternative, or can even use the best of both approaches if they so wish. As trust in the non-linear approach develops, an artist will naturally find a personal style.

Paola Paronetto (Italy), collection of bottles, 2009. Paperclay porcelain, height: 30–90 cm (11¾–35½ in.). *Photo: Willy Friend.*

The linear approach

Artists may work in paperclay with minimal changes to the established routines and work habits they use with traditional clay. These practical and proven linear methods have evolved over millennia of experience.

Traditional clay, when dry but unfired, can be extremely fragile and vulnerable to cracks. To compensate for this, the transition between wet and dry stages requires a set of one-way steps. It requires the artist to hold all the parts of the structure at the damp and leatherhard stage until assembly, carving, joining and trimming processes are complete, after which the finished assembly must be allowed to dry as evenly and slowly as possible. The more complex the form, the more attention must be paid to this. An even dampness is maintained by various imaginative means, whether by swaddling the work in damp rags, enclosing the work in a tent of plastic wrap, periodic water spraying, or by leaving the work in a humidified damp room between work periods. To dry and fire the work successfully, a consistent, even wall thickness is needed also. These traditional rules and approaches can be followed when working with paperclay, with some variations, described throughout this book (see also p. 155).

For an example of working by the linear system, a form started from a solid lump of traditional clay is kept at a leatherhard, damp state during the process of hollowing and removing excess softer clay from the interior, to make the walls an even thickness before a period of slow drying begins. But those who want to adapt this method for

LEFT: Sue Stewart (Australia), *Gallery Scenario*, 2011. Scale model in paperclay, 32 x 32 x 24 cm (12½ x 12½ x 9½ in.). *Photo: Sue Stewart.*

ABOVE: Rosette Gault (USA), *Littlefoot and Chew Toy*, 2009. Pinched figure in porcelain paperclay, 9 x 7.5 x 6.5 cm (3½ x 3 x 2½ in.). *Photo: Rosette Gault.*

paperclay find it easier to hollow out the interior while it is soft as paste and the outside shell has started to harden. Leatherhard (or dry) paperclay can also be re-softened by soaking with a damp rag or worked wet over dry. The interiors of large-scale, complex, leatherhard paperclay projects could take many months to dry using the traditional slow-drying system, but in medium- to high-pulp paperclay, the work can be dried in the open air in hours or a few days, or be force-dried, and walls can be uneven in thickness.

Some artists use small portions of paperclay to patch and repair cracks in traditional clay. Others add just a small amount of pulp to their clay, to gain a small increase in strength in the dry state for transport and loading in kilns. Some artists have invested many years in mastering and refining traditional methods with leatherhard and soft clay; they see no reason to give them up. Artists will find most clay and glaze techniques are compatible with or can be adapted for paperclay.

The non-linear approach

This approach involves artistic license and freedom to work beyond the leatherhard state, which exponentially expands the number of possibilities available to you. It may involve new work rhythms, the use of new moisture states, different timings and more chances for imagination. The time I used to spend trying to stop my sculpture from drying unevenly and compensating for fear of cracks is now freed up for creativity. Using the linear approach, I used to keep the entire work in progress and all its parts swaddled in wet towels or plastic during the entire sculpting period. The consequences of neglect with traditional clay were severe; if a work dried out or cracked, I would have to hammer it down and start over. The use of non-linear methods for paperclay, described throughout this book, ends the need for long drying and firing times, reduces losses occurring due to cracking and in transport, and allows for repairs to be made at dry and even fired stages. You will see some of the ways artists are using these new methods in the chapters that follow.

For me, the research process of testing the performance limits and working out the right recipe balances for functional paperclays led to a string of revelations. A high percentage of assumptions and practices needed in traditional ceramics do not apply for the non-linear approach with paperclay.

Kiln results always keep fantasy in check. The kiln will find any weakness an artist hasn't attended to, no matter what clay or approach is used. As I gradually came to understand the inner workings of paperclay, discussed in the next chapter, I came to understand weakness and strength in a new and harmonious way, so that my view of ceramics and art practice changed forever.

The imagination of paperclay artists who integrate non-linear methods into their practice extends far beyond the fundamental skills of well-documented traditional methods. As we look at the evolution and spirit behind the new and alternative practices throughout this book, an expanded view of the hands-on creation process will become possible.

Sabina Mangus (USA), pinched spoons and bowls, 2010. Hand-pinched porcelain paperclay, diameter: 10–20 cm (4–8 in.). *Photo: Sabina Mangus.*

2   Ingredients and mixing

The creation of small batches of high-quality paperclay in an artist's studio goes more smoothly when a plan, tools and appropriate set-up are in place, and ingredients are at the ready. Time spent getting a general understanding of these elements will make the decision easier as to which type of paperclay is best suited to your project or purpose.

Review the Health and Safety information in the Appendix (p. 144) before you begin working with paperclay.

Tools and work surfaces

All kinds of clay modelling and trimming tools – ribs, sponges, fettles, sticks, needles, wire, wheels, etc. – can be used with paperclay. In addition, artists sometimes borrow tools from wood- or metalworking, such as hand or power drills, saws and carving tools for working on dry paperclay.

Paperclay does not stick to most smooth table or countertop work surfaces unless it is extremely soft or wet – almost a paste. Sometimes paperclays will stick or dry too fast on canvas-covered worktables. The smooth surface of a tabletop works well. If the tabletop becomes wet or moist under the work area and paperclay starts to stick, transfer the project to a nearby dry spot on the table and resume.

A portable plaster work-surface will help to dry works in progress or paperclay slip more quickly. Prop it up on a set of blocks or rails so air can circulate underneath it. This all-purpose tool is an easy-to-store alternative to bulky slab-roller equipment.

LEFT: Astrid Heimer (Norway), *Horse Croquis*, 2011. Paperclay porcelain, 35 x 32 cm (13¾ x 12½ in.). *Photo: Eva Braend.*

RIGHT: Plaster slabs can be used as multipurpose work surfaces for drying, making flat and smooth paperclay slabs, wedging soft paperclay and more. These are propped up at the corners to ventilate below. *Photo: Rosette Gault.*

Tools for mixing

Reserve a set of clean, watertight mixing buckets with covering lids for the mixing process. I store these out of the way under a work table or in a corner.

A sink or water source nearby, as well as a power source, is helpful. A plug-in drill to mix thick slips will hold up better than battery-powered 'cordless' models. A propeller-style mixing-blade attachment, like that designed for drywall, cuts mixing time to a minimum and leads to less wear and tear on a drill than the type used to mix paint or liquid glaze, which is designed for more soupy liquid. When using power tools, be certain that cords are in good condition and that feet and hands remain dry at all times. The power supply should be switched off when you are cleaning the blade. Avoid letting a moving tool hit the bottom or sides of the bucket.

Whenever possible, mix ingredients wet to avoid producing dust. When mixing dry ingredients, use a breathing mask. I use goggles to protect from water/slip splash when mixing, or for checking the temperature inside a kiln. Keep a selection of many types of gloves to hand: leather, rubber, vinyl and latex. If my hands will be wet for hours, I use barrier hand creams.

Preparation of ingredients

There are three types of ingredients that combine to make a high-functioning paperclay: base clay, paper pulp and water. The process for making small or larger batches in an artist's studio will be quick when these key variables have been prepared ahead of time. You will also have more control and understanding when making adaptations and shortcuts for different projects or recipes. In this chapter we will discuss the function and preparation of each ingredient in paperclay.

Preparing a base clay

Most base clay recipes can be converted for paperclay. The base clay recipe you use might be, for example, a favourite recipe that you know is compatible with your glazes. High-grog sculpture clay recipes are an exception, as extra adjustments to the base clay are needed (explained pp. 20 and 148).

Nearly all clay types can serve as a base, including red or black terracotta, white or tan earthenware, brown or white stoneware, porcelain- or kaolin-based clay, or combinations of these. Whether the clay source is recycled slake-down from dried scrap, from the potter's slop bucket, gathered from a nearby riverbed or derived from dry powder, the slip should be the consistency of thick cream or smooth, thick cake icing. Lumpy base-clay slip will not mix easily with paper pulp. If you feel stubborn clay lumps in the mix, remove them before you start mixing a paperclay. The orphaned lumps would otherwise present difficulties later in wedging and drying, or may result in cracking, shearing or chipping during or after firing.

My mixing tools include: an assortment of bucket sizes (for pulp, clay, paperclay slip, dry scrap reclaim); covered, watertight barrels set on low-wheeled dollies (which make it easy to move, fill, empty and/or store them); a heavy-duty power drill tool with a plug-in propeller mixing blade; and a sink or water source nearby. You can also see a mesh bag used for straining pulp draped over one of the lids. *Photo: Rosette Gault.*

When 'beating' paper back to pulp, a rod and propeller tool saves time because the blades have more surface area. Attach it securely to a power drill. To speed the process up even more, be very generous with water. *Photo: Rosette Gault.*

Another type of suitable base clay is well-stirred casting slip. This has a heavy, honey-like consistency formulated for easy pouring into moulds. It contains dispersal agents/electrolytes (sodium silicate, soda ash, Darvan 7 or equivalent). Casting slip can be adapted as a base for special end-use ceramic paperclay, such as cast panels or sheets, bone china, figurines, factory sanitary, and computer-modelled or machined prototypes.

Whichever type of base you start with, the paperclay version will shrink in drying and firing by about the same amount, on average only 1% less than the parent clay. The fired porosity of a paperclay can vary from the porosity of its base clay by, on average, between 1 and 5% when the variable of temperature and base clay is constant. However, I and other researchers have found and tested paperclays that fire to a watertight or vitreous non-porous condition (see also endnote 2 on p. 27).

Faults in poor batches of base clay will not be corrected in a paperclay version. Like traditional clay, crumbling, bloating and low tensile strength will be evident after firing. If you have made a bad batch by mistake, it may be faster to just make a new, good batch. Clay body adjustment is beyond the scope of this book. Nevertheless, the chart on p. 149 offers details about selection of man-made fibres that can be combined with paperclay recipes for advanced practice. Firing paperclay will be discussed in Chapter 11, since optimum vitrification temperatures for the paperclay version of a base clay may shift up or down a few cones in your part of the world (10–50°C, or 50–122°F).

Sandra Black (Australia), *Hardenbergia*, 2011. Cast, carved, pierced and polished ebony mix of porcelain, with black colourant added into the paperclay slip, 15.2 x 26.4 cm (6 x 10½ in.). *Photo: courtesy of Sabbia Gallery, Paddington, Sydney.*

Paperclay for sculpture

Great sculpture paperclay can be made from a base slip that is very smooth with no grit in it at all. Recipes for sculpture paperclay using this type of base clay are on pp. 148 and 158. Commercially-prepared sculpture clays, the exception to the base-clay conversion rules, can feature a very rough and sandy surface. It is likely that the maximum possible amount of non-clay 'filler' – such as grog, chamotte, sand, perlite or vermiculite – is already present in the base clay, because traditional sculpture clay requires these ingredients as stabilisers.

Cellulose fibre is also a non-clay filler. If you add pulp to a grog-filled base clay, the ratio of filler to clay can be too high. Too much filler in a base clay recipe ultimately weakens the tensile strength of the ceramic. The result, no matter what the firing temperature, can be crumbly after firing.

There are various remedies for this. If it is not possible to change the base clay – for instance, if the paperclay slip you have is based on a reclaimed, high-texture 'sculpture clay' – match every measure of pulp you add with a double or triple measure of plastic clay, such as ball clay or kaolin, to bring back the balance of clay to filler. If you need to do this, blend the extra clay into high-grog paperclay slip first before adding the pulp, and ensure to test-fire a small smaple.

Recycled paper as fibre source

Papers made from cotton, linen, flax and soft and hard wood are the principal sources of cellulose fibre suitable for adding to clay (see pp. 145–6, 149). Though virgin cellulose fibre could be used, the majority of household papers contain some form of cellulose fibre, which we turn back to pulp by mixing in water. Vegetable- or soy-based inks on reclaimed paper or newsprint will burn away during firing.

As the source of cellulose is a living plant, each paper fibre is a complex spiral containing a DNA structure. The paperclay mix is, therefore, a form of 'bio-ceramic'. The dynamic internal structure of the cellulose in paperclay is discussed later in this chapter (p. 24).

Fibre of all kinds has long been added to building materials to increase tensile strength. It has been argued that manmade fibres (nylon, dacron, and the like) are functionally interchangeable with or even superior to pulp, since they can be of uniform diameter and length and do not absorb water. While it is true that manmade refractory ceramic fibres do not burn, and contribute to fired tensile strength when mixed in base-clay bodies, they lack water absorbency and other attributes that cellulose fibres offer. There is a certain dynamic interaction between water, cellulose fibre and clay in a paperclay body, which doesn't happen if manmade fibre is substituted. The three classes of fibre are compared in the Appendix (p. 149).

Convert recycled paper to a pulp of cellulose fibre

To recycle your own paper and turn it into pulp for paperclay, there are a few steps to follow. Depending on the tools, the paper, the amount of water and its temperature, this process could take from less than five minutes to several hours. In practice, few studio artists recycle papers when doing their first test mixes, since toilet paper is an easy, available option, dispersing quickly by hand, even in cold water (see p. 23).

Gather and sort papers to recycle

When preparing papers for your paper pulp, grade and sort them for quality, type and ease of tearing. Papers with a matt surface, with simple ink, and which are easy to tear or shred even when dry, will take less time to turn into pulp. These include most forms of newsprint, household or office computer papers, egg cartons and the like. Avoid the types known to need more time to break down into pulp, such as cardstock, cardboard (containing glues) or craft paper. A chart listing suitable paper sources is included in the Appendix (p. 146). Identify a reliable and consistent source of paper to recycle. This will enable more control over repeat batches and recipe adjustments.

Ensure to remove envelope windows, cellophane, wax, plastic, glue and staples, as these do not break apart easily in water. Staples and paperclips usually cause a dark mark when fired and are dangerous for wedging. Most soy printer inks do not affect the fired ceramic colour. Some heavy metal inks will lend a tan or darker tint to the fired clay. Do a test firing of your paperclay to check if a possible colour change is a concern.

Mix paper pulp

Fill a large bucket three-quarters up with water. Warm or hot water speeds up the process for most pulps. Dip a medium handful of shredded paper in the water. Alternatively, dip a toilet roll and soak it well so that it pulls apart easily, then remove the cardboard centre. Agitate by hand or with a power tool until the paper has broken down; you are aiming for a thin soup of pulp water. The image below left shows what shredded newsprint can look like as pulp.

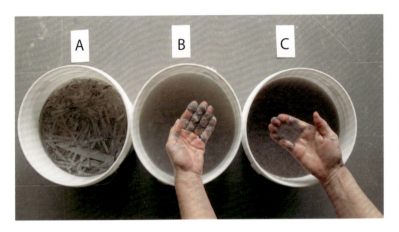

Ink from thin, torn strips of recycled newspaper will turn the pulp and water 'soup' a dark grey. The paper in bucket A has not broken down enough; in bucket B, wet paper bits are still visible in the water. Continue mixing until all the paper has been converted to pulp, as seen in bucket C, before straining. With newsprint or shredded paper, the process can take half an hour or more. *Photo: Gayle St Luise.*

Once no flecks of paper are visible, wet pulp can be gathered by pouring the mixture through a household sieve. You can check for flecks by looking at a small amount in a clear drinking glass. *Photo: Betsy Nield.*

A single roll of toilet paper quickly yields this volume of pulp, even in cold water – more than enough for a small test batch of paperclay. *Photo: Rosette Gault.*

RIGHT: An alternative to sieving is to pour the pulp soup through a mesh bag. Drain, but don't squeeze out too much water. *Photo: Melissa Grace Miller.*

The paper should be soaked and beaten for long enough that the fibres separate and flecks of paper disappear. It helps to know beforehand what a broken-down paper pulp will look like, both in the pulp water and after it has been loosely strained, and be aware that some papers take less effort to dipserse into pulp fibre than others (see p. 146). For a simple preview, vigorously swish a small handful of toilet paper in a medium-size bowl of water for a few minutes by hand. Strain wet fibres from the water with a kitchen sieve, or pour the pulp soup through in a mesh bag. Strained, wet pulp is ready to measure and mix with clay slip.

Leave the pulp wet. If you squeeze too much water out of the cellulose fibre, hard wads of pulp form and these don't disperse well in the clay slip (see p. 152). They will show up as visible lumps in the clay that will, in due course, fire out as voids.

Dry blends of 'fluff' from recycled paper, like the kind often used for stuffing padded envelopes or found at a building supply store for insulation, may not be the shortcut they seem to be. If these are used in a paperclay mix, flecks of unpulped paper will be visible, and these leave large pocks and voids when they fire out. Dry blends of pulp also generate dust. Unless your studio kiln is truly well-ventilated and located in a rural area, avoid using dry recycled fluff (see also pp. 134, 144 and 152).

Fire retardants are often added to bags of dry blends in some countries. Normal untreated paper takes approximately two to three hours to burn off in a kiln at very low temperature, but papers treated with fire retardants can continue to smoke at bisque temperatures and higher, with foul-smelling fumes that are toxic to inhale.

Balance of pulp to clay

Acceptable ratios between pulp and clay for paperclay are easily calculated by volume, and mixed when wet. A mix of wet ingredients creates conditions in which the tiniest clay particles will be drawn in and trapped in the rough edges of each cellulose fibre. This may affect the fired properties of special-purpose paperclay mixes currently being researched. Shortcuts, variations and adaptations are possible once you gain experience with the medium.

Enough cellulose fibre is needed to create a uniform, flexible, internal lattice of fibre, embedded in and separated by clay particles. As a result of this internal network, water or air will flow throughout the dry or bisque paperclay until it is fired to a vitreous temperature and/or sealed with glaze. The function of such a structure mimics capillaries, which allow circulation within human tissues, or plant root systems. The apertures of the hollow cellulose fibres will swell up just a bit when wet and shrink back again when dry.

Cellulose and clay shrink at a near-equivalent rate. Paperclay forms thus remain more or less intact and stable, despite the cycle of change between wet to dry. Although cellulose fibre may burn away during the fire, my research suggests that, in a majority of mixes, the narrow hollows remain within the clay, much like the remains left by a fossil, so the internal structure continues to mitigate any thermal or moisture stress experienced after firing. Weather, temperature and moisture changes could cause the

BELOW: Handling the wet toilet roll.
Photo: Melissa Grace Miller.

volume of some fired paperclays to continue to expand or contract slightly, but they will remain intact over years (see p. 129).

There are lots of ways in which cellulose fibre contributes to the stability of paperclay ceramic before and after firing. Cellulose is, at the molecular level, a spiral structure made up of tightly-wound coils, which flex, stretch and compress with surprising tensile strength in many directions (see below). Because of these tiny spirals, high-pulp paperclay may feel slightly springy in the hand when soft and sheets of it may flex a bit when dry.

Each cellulose fibre likewise resembles a water-absorbent, tapered drinking straw. The internal lattice of cellulose fibre permits moisture and air to move easily through the dry paperclay. During the process of burnishing a paperclay surface, openings in the cellulose can be compressed from a round shape to oval or flat. Moisture and air cannot flow through flattened fibres; those who wedge or knead prefer soft over stiff mix for this reason.

At a closer level of magnification we now know that each cellulose fibre is also sheathed in a network of still smaller nano-fibres. The smallest clay particles in a clay body recipe are also nano-sized. During the mixing, many of these will become embedded between, in and around the nano-fibres. When certain compounds of paperclay are fired to a temperature at which the carbon turns to a gas and exits the clay, many nano-sized voids remain within the ceramic. Some high-pulp paperclay can then function as a nano-sized porous material that can be shaped or modelled as desired. My early-stage research shows promise for water filtration and other applications.[1] *Innovation in Paperclay Ceramic Arts* (Gault 2013) supplies additional formal academic perspective on aesthetic and technical contribution to the field, background and development history for researchers in the field.

Those who want paperclay to be vitreous or watertight can achieve this.[2] There are base clay or glaze combinations containing minerals that, when placed in the fire, will melt and seal the tiny 'nano-sized' voids otherwise left after firing, at the precise temperature desired. Refinements of specialty paperclay ceramics are in development.

Every type of cellulose fibre is in essence a flexible, water-absorbent helix. Here, I have modelled some paperclay coils to give a sense of the dynamic shapes and structures of cellulose fibre. *Photo: Gayle St Luise.*

ABOVE LEFT: Adding pulp to clay slip. Fill the bucket up partway and mark the level with a stick or ruler. Add a volume of pulp up to that mark and the level will rise. Mark the new level and stir. Use the same bucket and stick for each batch, for the purpose of comparison. *Photo: Rosette Gault.*

ABOVE RIGHT: Informal mixing by eye for small amounts like this is common, since paperclay slip is best used freshly made. This paperclay slip will make an all-purpose patch that seals cracks over most traditional clay, as well as paperclay. *Photo: Melissa Grace Miller.*

Mixing pulp and clay

Stir measures of wet paper pulp into a container of measures of smooth base-clay slip using your hand, a paddle or a rotary mixing blade on a drill. In the photo on the next page, you will see a range of possible choices, from high to low pulp mixes. Each pulp-to-clay ratio has a slightly different purpose: the details of these ratios are described in the Appendix (pp. 147–8). You can measure by units of volume or keep track by marking the side of your mixing bucket.

Wet mix measures

Because each type of recycled paper will vary in the speed at which it breaks down into pulp, its water absorbency, fibre length and many other characteristics, advice to measure fibre or paper just by weight can be less helpful. The volume of pulp from one type of cellulose can be exchanged for the same volume of another type of cellulose fibre, in general.[3] So a volume of shredded newsprint or computer paper could be substituted for a volume of pulp sourced from toilet rolls that might be described in a paperclay recipe. Students marvel at the variations in yields of pulp between different brands of toilet paper. Measuring volume when wet will minimise airborne dust in the workspace, too, and this method can be adapted to any size of container.

Do test-fire your result to confirm that the base clay looks and feels as you expect. For consistent results, make notes and use the same-size buckets and the same ingredients in the same amounts.

A simple way to measure volume is to put a ruler or stick into the mixing bucket of clay slip, mark the level, then add pulp so that the level rises on the ruler to the new mark desired (see photo above left). I use the same size buckets and stick/ruler each time. Do not fuss over the exact proportions if, for example, you are short of prepared pulp or mistakenly added a lot more than intended. It may be simplest just to use what you have mixed, test-fire a sample, learn from it and make amends in the next batch.

Sculpture
Ratios 1:3 to 1:5

HIGH-PULP FOR
LIGHTWEIGHT

MAXIMUM, VERY
LIGHTWEIGHT

RECIPE
VARIATIONS
MEASURE PARTS
OF WET PULP
TO CLAY SLIP BY
VOLUME.

Pulp-to-clay guide. Measure volume proportions with the same size container for both wet pulp and thick clay base slip. The higher the pulp to-clay ratio, the lighter the weight after firing and a better wet to dry join or patch. If too little pulp is added, wet-to-dry joins will fail. Base clays added rough texture of grog or sand are not recommended.

Clays and pulps vary by region so a range of volume recipes are shown. The Appendix (pp. 147–8) contains full details and end purposes for each. For instance on the left is a more clay like feel of 1 part pulp: 3 parts slip mix. The middle shows slightly more putty like feel of 1 pulp: 2 clay ratio. To right is a lightweight mix of 1 part pulp: 1 part thick slip, which might be used for patch (p. 25), lightweight sculptures, tile, interior filler (p. 94), casting, and modeling.
Photo: Gayle St Luise.

Recipe guidelines

Artists have infinite choices in adjusting base-clay ingredients, the amount of water and the amount of pulp. For casual projects or student trials, one might start by informally stirring in the pulp until the paperclay slip looks like oatmeal, thus skipping the exact measuring that professionals would use. But in fact all the attributes of ceramic – weight, density, colour, tensile strength, hardness, porosity and texture – can be regulated to a very high degree for any purpose desired.

Recipes are described at greater length in the Appendix, pp. 147–8. Refer to this for guidance with a favorite clay/glaze combination.

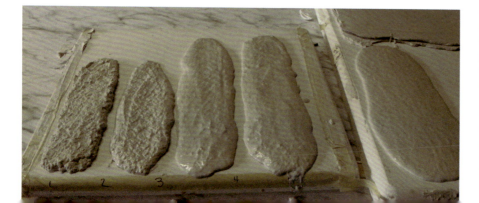

Paperclay slip surface texture can be adjusted as desired either changing water or pulp amount. Some pulp to clay volume ratio mixes poured out on a plaster drying surface from left to right to compare are: 1:1; 1:2; 1:3; 1:4; 1:5. Some ways to turn fresh mix paperclay slips like these into wedged modelling paperclay consistency are explained in photos on p. 43.
Photo: Rosette Gault.

Malene Pedersen (Denmark), *Bowl*, 1996. A thin-walled, dry paperclay pinch pot is strong enough to handle when it is dry. In traditional clay, it would be too fragile. *Photo: Malene Pedersen.*

Maria Gellert (Spain), *Bowl*, 2004. This blue paperclay porcelain contains a high concentrate of cobalt blue stain in the base recipe. Coloured paperclays can be coated with a transparent glaze for a gloss finish, diameter: 46 cm (18 in.). *Photo: Rosette Gault.*

Compatibility between paperclays

High- and low-pulp paperclay can usually be attached or laminated together in the same project. The base clays are typically the same. If base clays are different colours or types, make sure the firing temperatures of each are compatible. For large-scale sculpture, I may use a very high-pulp mix as reinforcement inside a figure sculpture that needs thick yet lightweight sections under the arms or wings or at other intersecting structural joins (see photos on pp. 67, 95 and 98).

Many artists ask if they can join paperclay to traditional clay. The general rule is to use the rules of traditional clay when traditional clay predominates the project (leatherhard joins, and paperclay for patch repairs) and to use the new paperclay rules (dry-to-dry and dry-to-wet joins) when paperclay predominates. Smaller-sized traditional clay parts that are already dry or fired can be inserted and worked into wet paperclay. Example works can be seen in Chapter 3 (top right, p. 30) and Chapter 9 (p. 109).

Endnotes

1. Gault, R 2010, *The Potential of Paperclay Ceramic in Water Filtration a Case Study in Nicaragua*, presented to Ceramic Art and Sustainable Society, Gothenberg, Sweden. Published in three parts in June 2011, *Ceramics Art and Perception: Technical*, Issue 31, June 2011, Issue 32, Fall 2011, to Issue 32, May 2012.
2. Gault Report, *Tests for Water Absorption and Shrinkage of Multiple Clays Compared to Paperclays* (unpublished document), 1995.
3. See chart in the Appendix (p. 145) to see how pulps compare in cellulose content.

3 Paperclay slip

The liquid form of paperclay is called paperclay slip in this book, but 'paperslip', 'paperclay slurry' or 'p'slip' are other names you might hear. The commercial blend is known as P'Slip®. Paperclay slip is versatile throughout the creation process. As water evaporates, it gradually thickens to modelling consistency and will air-harden.

Methods for using paperclay slip involve practices from both ceramics and mixed media. It can be a sticky adhesive, surface coating or gap filler. Its texture can be thin like soup, thicker like oatmeal porridge, or thicker still, like a paste, whipped cream or mashed potatoes. It can be applied as a topcoat for a surface treatment – sprayed, brushed, dipped and trailed. Layers of paperclay slip can be built up to increase depth, texture and colour. The slip can be stained or tinted in a variety of fire-friendly colours. It is commonly used to to patch and repair over dry or bisque paperclay, and serves as grout over and around dry, bisque or glazed ceramic mosaic or additions. It can also be cast in a variety of moulds.

Paperclay slip appeals to the imagination of artists who want to integrate methods from sculpture and mixed media with ceramic process. For example, small pieces of fired ceramic may be integrated in a large wall panel of freshly-made paperclay slip, as shown in the photo on the next page, or slip can be applied in a painterly way with engobes, texture and glazes.

LEFT: Rebecca Hutchinson (USA), *Holter Installation*, 2008. Unfired paperclay porcelain. *Photo: Holter Museum, Montana, USA.*

RIGHT: Rosette Gault (USA), *Flight*, 2012. Porcelain paperclay wall works exhibited in Seattle in the Nordstrom's window March–April, 3 x 2 m (10 x 5 ft.) *Photo: Rosette Gault.*

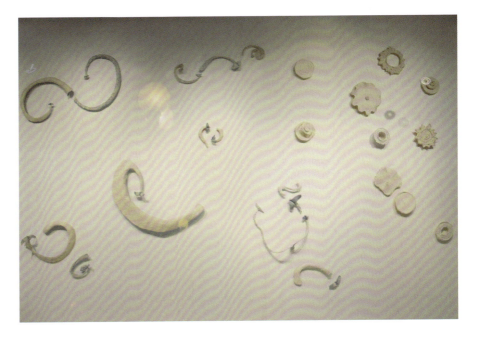

If you have poured more paperclay slip than you need onto a plaster slab or into a mould, return any excess to the bucket. *Photo: Melissa Grace Miller.*

Press dry, cast, bisque, glazed or fired ceramic forms into a freshly poured thick puddle of high-pulp slip on a plaster slab. The slip will dry and hold them in place through firing too. *Photo: Gayle St Luise.*

Care of paperclay slip

Once you have mixed paperclay slip, as described in Chapter 2, it will look like a thick porridge in the bucket. After it settles overnight, sponge or decant excess water off the top. If the mix is left uncovered in the bucket, it thickens over time. The time it takes depends on how much water you used, the temperature and the humidity in the air. Stir the mix periodically, every day or so.

Moisture in the paperclay slip can be regulated to achieve the consistency desired. If the mix turns too thick, stir in some water. Use fresh-made studio paperclay slip within a week or two, when possible. If it dries in the bucket due to neglect, it can be reclaimed.

Read more about storage and aging of paperclays in the Appendix (pp. 144, 153).

Paperclay slip as adhesive

Use paperclay slip as a glue between paperclay in all moisture states (leatherhard, dry, bisque, sometimes even fired). The bond between dry-to-dry sections is quite often more secure than a bond with leatherhard parts. The traditional practice of pre-scoring a texture at the points of contact to increase surface area before applying slip is necessary for weight-bearing joins with paperclay. This is, however, optional with other types of join. New methods for bonds and joins between dry/wet, dry/dry and dry/wet/dry will be shown in the chapters that follow. One example can be been seen on p. 33, with a fresh, soft coil being added to the rim of a dry pot. A bead of paperclay slip for the glue is visible along the seam line, just after both parts have been pressed together.

Paperclay slip bonds with almost all porous, semi-porous, matt and semi-matt surfaces. It sticks securely to dry paperclay, under-fired paperclay, bisque, soft or hard firebrick or mason's brick. Paperclay slip also sticks well to other porous materials, such as natural fabrics, paper, cardboard and wood. For non-porous gloss surfaces, like glass or glazed ceramics, thin coats of paperclay slip can often be brushed or sprayed over them to give a weak, temporary bond before firing. If the assembly is fired to the right temperature, the coating of paperclay slip will bond in place.

Paperclay slip as sealant or coating

Apply paperclay slip over dry coils to seal in moments, as shown in the image below.

The exterior of the demonstration bowl shows some finished effects between single and multiple layers of paperclay slip over the dry coils, when the coating was applied by fan brush. The more coatings, the less coil contour will be seen. Paperclay slip functions here as both adhesive and surface coating. As mentioned, the traditional practice of roughing up the surface and applying slip for joining is optional for paperclay, and can in many instances be skipped. Very soft, fresh-made coils can be quickly set to dry in any position (see p. 10). At the dry stage, a coating of thin paperclay slip neatly joins the coils and sets in minutes.

It is a new practice in ceramics to wait till the dry state to do joins and there are several practical benefits. Coils that are dry and hard are less vulnerable to dents or fingerprints than soft or leatherhard coils. The visible pattern of carefully-placed soft coils is often worth keeping. If there is sufficient pulp in the paperclay slip, there will be few or no drying cracks to patch when the join dries. Repeat the patching process or change your paperclay slip recipe if cracks between the coils persist.

To seal between dry coils, coat them with layers of paperclay slip. Seal the coils on the inside first, wait until this dries, then lift the coiled bowl out intact. In the background, you can see the glass bowl that was used to support the soft paperclay coils during building, acting as a temporary 'nest' until the coils hardened completely. The lines of the coils will be preserved; should you want to smooth between the coils, add layers of slip to build up thickness. Spraying vegetable oil on the bowl will aid early release of not-quite-dry coils, though this is optional. *Photo: Gayle St Luise.*

Paperclay slip for repair and patch

Of all the repair skills to master with paperclay, larger cracks are relatively easy for first timers. Apply thin paperclay slip over and around dry cracks to fill them (note that paperclay slip does not soak quite as deeply into leatherhard cracks as it does into dry cracks). The slip will soak deepest into dry cracks and the excess can be trimmed with a blade or wiped clean with a damp sponge. For a gap filler, I might apply a thick paste of paperclay slip in the gap after. Dry this completely in the open air or in a warm place.

For patches, paperclay slip works best between paperclays, but many use it to patch non-paperclay ceramic, too. This is the way many traditional clay artists were introduced to the medium of paperclay. We saw how to mix a quick paperclay slip for patch on p. 25.

For a big crack, I typically wipe down the dry paperclay with a wet sponge beforehand, in a wide area (5-10 cm/2-4 in.) around the crack (see pp. 63–4). This extra surface water will evaporate fairly quickly on the dry ware, but prepares the surface for the patch.

Artists can sometimes patch bisque cracks as well. Bisque is porous under-fired clay or paperclay, fired to about cone 04. The bisque repair method is a little different than the dry method. Wet the bisque first, then apply a thin coating of paperclay slip. It seems best to allow this initial thin layer to dry before applying more layers; subsequent layers can be thicker. A putty or thick paste of paperclay slip fills gaps, too. After the repair dries, fire the new join at a high bisque temperature (cone 04) again to test it. If cracks persist, repeat the process. The dipped bandage-style patch discussed in the next section can be adapted for bisque in a similar way. Bisque repair with paperclay slip has a 50% chance of success, compared to 98% with repair over dry paperclay. Hairline cracks can be a special challenge. Bisque cracks are further discussed on pp. 64 and 78.

The subject of patch and repair is vast. Artists adapt and merge methods from other disciplines such as auto-body repair, building trades, fabric tailoring, textiles and others. In the Appendix you will find some illustrations of how the repair process can often transform a weakness into a strength (p. 147).

Slip for internal reinforcement and filler

Dip strips or cut-outs of paperclay, of any size, texture, shape or condition, in paperclay slip. Then apply these as patches or bandages, internally or externally, to the work in progress. Most patches stick in seconds to dry paperclay if the slip is thin. If your slip is very thick, remoisten the dry paperclay a few moments before you apply it.

Reinforcement methods with paperclay slip can be handy for larger-scale projects involving dry paperclay. Projects that need an internal structure, such as a cross-bracing of paperclay tubes, would be typical. When assembling dry parts, thick high-pulp slip can be built up in layers several inches thick, inside, outside, over or under the dry parts of the internal structure. To get an idea of how a thick application of slip will dry, you can compare some cross-section views on p. 98.

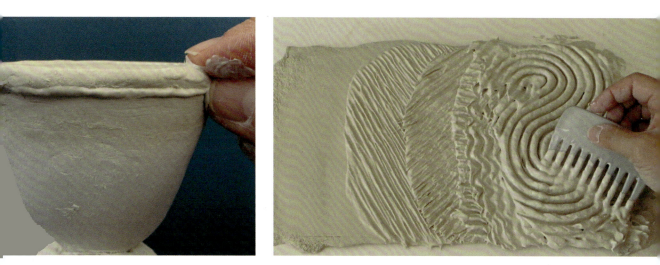

To reinforce a join that could use a measure of fired tensile strength beyond that of just the base clay, dip a speciality fibre that is refractory – such as fibreglass-weave cloth, refractory fibre blanket or alumina fibre – in a paperclay slip, then apply it to the form.

Control the 'grain' and add new texture to paperclay slip

We see new surfaces and textures in ceramics today, which have evolved from imaginative experiments with paperclay slip. For example, wood and some kinds of paper have a 'grain', and in paperclay an artist can manage the predominant direction of the cellulose fibres to create a similar effect.

Before a pool of paperclay slip hardens, it can be stirred with your fingers, a serrated rib, a fork, a comb or some other tool. Texture from this process may or may not be visible on the surface of the fresh pour on top, but deep inside the slip, the three-dimensional lattice of cellulose fibre will be rearranged. I use this method when making large, high-pulp, flat wall panels, but it can be adapted after dipping in slip also, discussed in the next part of this chapter. It's also easy to create a laminate of poured layers of paperclay slip, like plywood. A laminate effect can be integrated with a repair or reinforcement to a structural join.

Paperclay pools and thick pastes

Thick or thin puddles and pools of paperclay slip can be poured to achieve surface textures like paper, porridge, water, a whirlpool, a river, cresting waves, cake icing, hairy tufts and numerous others (see pp. 114–5 and 117 for more surface effects). Coats of high-pulp slip will normally dry intact without any cracks. For intentional cracking-up textures in drying, reduce the amount of pulp in the recipe. Some artists stir extra burn-out media, such as coconut fibre, seeds, rice, noodles and sawdust, into paperclay slip, applying the resulting mixture as a thick or thin paste to their chosen surface.

Coating and dipping with slip

Surface coating with paperclay appeals to a wide range of artists, even those with no ceramic experience. It is a quick way to transform the appearance of nearly any object. It has been adopted for unfired paperclay since so many types of media are compatible with it. Many practices traditionally used with other sculpture media, like wax, metals, and glass, are integrated by artists who are familiar with firing in kilns; likewise, paperclay practices have been adopted by artists and sculptors who do not typically use ceramic kilns.

Though paperclay slip can be applied by spraying, brushing or sponging, dipping is also popular. Artists dip a wide range of media: paper sheets, cardboard cut-outs, poster board, boxes, strings, twine, rope, tree branches, twigs, wood, leaves, organic sponges, food and plants, coconut fibre, clothing, shoes, noodles, seeds, wood, crumpled or wadded paper, wax and more. These give surface textures not previously seen in ceramics. These special surface effects combine with glaze and firing practices such as raku, reduction, metallic glazes and lustres.

Typically, the dipped object needs at least three coats of paperclay slip to build up enough wall thickness to be strong after firing, when the dipped organic part will burn out. Wait between dips, either for the coating to stiffen slightly or for it to dry

Dip paper cut-outs in paperclay slip multiple times to build up a thick coating, waiting for the dipped shape to dry between each dipping. Re-wetting will soften up the dry paperclay cut-out for modelling and you can assemble the parts when dry. Rebecca Hutchinson (USA), work in progress, 2008. *Photo: Rosette Gault.*

The artist Helen Gilmour from UK soaks her 100% cotton knitting in porcelain slip and builds up layers in stages. Gilmour adds "Work dried out on an inflated balloon. It takes several days of soaking, coating, and drying to reach this stage when I am sure there is enough slip built up in layers to result in a strong ceramic pot after fire. The cotton all burns off in the firing process. I fire to 1280C". *Photo: Helen Gilmour.*

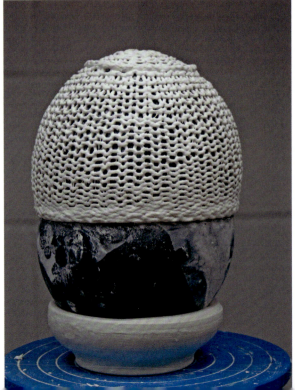

Thérèse LeBrun (Belgium) dips a nylon hosiery bag filled with soft stuffing in paperclay slip. To build up wall thickness, let the coating harden or dry between dips. At the end, dip in dry organic material (rice, seeds) or another material that will stick, or place a mosaic of material by hand, to dry in place. A final dip is optional. When dry, pull the stuffing from the bag and a thin shell with a special surface remains. *Photo: Paul Gruszow.*

A twig has burned out of a paperclay coating, leaving a hollow shell after firing. These can be assembled after the paperclay slip dries, or at bisque stage. Be sure there are enough layers of paperclay slip or the fired result will be too fragile to handle. Also make sure your kiln is properly ventilated. *Photo: Myra Toth (USA).*

completely. Some artists, such as Graham Hay, dip long lengths of rope in paperclay slip and tie it between trees like a clothesline to dry, cutting the hard, dry result to size afterwards. Dipped string, too, is becoming it its own specialty with which to build and an alternative to coiled clay. Dip natural-fibre string and yarn in paperclay slip to build up thick layers like a candle. Fresh coated string will not stand by itself and clings to porous surfaces, as well as dry or bisque paperclays. Lay or drape this over an easy-release plaster surface or balloon, or hang in mid-air until is strong enough to stand upright. The dry, coated string will bend in ways reminiscent of wire. More variations with dipped string can be found on p. 96.

When objects such as twigs are dipped in paperclay slip, the twigs burn out in firing, leaving the coating as a thin, hollow, ceramic shell (see above right). Often these forms will stimulate fresh points of view and delight the maker during the creation process, because they can be combined, stacked, and assembled in infinite variations.

A coating of paperclay slip can transform the exterior of dry forms or assemblies of paperclay in still more ways. Where dry paperclay is thin, moisture will re-soften the dry, hard part underneath, just enough to move it into a new position.

Firing dipped organic material

Burn-out of dipped organic material such as grasses, leaves, tree branches, flowers, cones, papers, cardboard and wads of crumpled paper gives off a form of smoke that kiln ventilation systems are designed for. A modest amount of this smoke is probably OK in a private studio. Be aware of the risks and precautions needed for successful

ABOVE: Marie Chantelot (Belgium) coats tiny bones and shrimp in a thin layer of paperclay slip. After the first coat is totally dry, she applies another to build up delicate porcelain shells and assemblies. *Photo: Paul Hasquine.*

LEFT: Miguel Angel Padilla Gomez (Mexico) coats a metal birdcage, with paperclay forms inside it, in a large bucket full of paperclay slip. Allow a little time between dips for the coating to set, before dipping again to build up layers. In addition to dry or fired paperclay, you can dip many other materials, including metal, but metal dipping is not advised for beginners and school studios due to risk of toxic fumes being emitted during firing. *Photo: Miguel Angel Padilla Gomez.*

Anthony Foo (USA), *Trapped*, 2009. Fired, paperclay-coated chickenwire frame with hand-built additions, 76 x 35.5 cm (30 x 14 in.). *Photo: Anthony Foo.*

firing of these materials, as described in Chapter 11 (p. 134) and in the Appendix (pp. 145, 152). Artists such as LeBrun and Tripaldi advise that most seeds fire well, except kernels of corn, which expand to 'popcorn' during the burn-out time.

Caution for metals and mixed media

Some artists push soft paperclay into a wire frame or dip metals in slip to get a flexing structure or frame to work over. This has been liberating for many practitioners and gives the surface a 'ceramic' look, compared to the more limited range of patina or other coatings available for metals. Although coating metals and man-made material with paperclay slip and firing them is convenient and fast, be aware that burn-out fumes are different than the ceramic fumes kiln ventilation systems are designed for. Those who fire paperclay-coated metals, such as chicken wire, wire mesh, hardware mesh, scrap metals, hardware, cast or wrought iron, or wires (copper and others) do so in well-ventilated studios only.

Dipping man-made materials such as soft and hard foams, Styrofoam, latex rubber, sponges, plastic bags, cups, or plastics is not recommended for projects that will be fired in the kiln. In many urban areas, these items (even if clay-coated) are considered hazardous waste.

Before modern paperclay, soft oil-based clay, plasticine or wax was often modelled over metal or wooden stick figures in sculpture classes. Some paperclay artists borrow this frame idea for supporting soft paperclay or paperclay slip. A coating of paperclay

Lorri Acott (USA),
Conversation with Myself,
2008. Raku-fired paperclay
with metal armature,
height: 40.5 cm (16 in.).
Photo: Rick Ney.

slip won't chip off when dry, the way that traditional clay casting slip tends to do.

Lorri Acott (USA) reports that dipped, large-sized, galvanised metals are very much less stable in fire than other metals, like stainless steel or iron, but that thin types of galvanised wire dipped in paperclay slip are fine. A number of speciality wires (e.g. nichrome wire) are still pliant after being subjected to a high temperature in a kiln.

Most metals have some affinity with paperclay slip. The degree of affinity after firing will depend in large part on the minerals in the base-clay body of the slip. High-sodium base-clay slips are among the many mixes being researched.

Caution and forethought is advised from the beginning when firing dipped items, as well as consideration for neighbours, animals and children. Be aware of health and safety needs, as well as the disposal of studio waste containing these items, particularly in urban areas.

Building with paperclay slip

Paperclay slip can be dribbled or trailed, as well as squirted in ribbons like icing, with 'piping' tools like those used by cooks for decoration and embellishment. For a make-do tool, squeeze slip into a plastic or cloth bag with one corner snipped off, as shown below. A dry 'slip trail' can stand on edge after it is dry and be used as a component in a sculpture or wall work. Antonella Cimatti has developed a method of filling a veterinary syringe with paperclay slip to paint thin lines on plaster, which release like a casting when dry. See an example of her lacy porcelain forms on p. 143, and her process below.

Squeezing a bag with the bottom corner cut open, Antonella Cimatti (Italy) trails thick paperclay slip in a large, open-face plaster mould. Paperclay slip trails are strong enough to stand upright on edge after they dry. Collaboration in progress between Antonella Cimatti and Rosette Gault. *Photo: Rolando Giovannini.*

Paperclay porcelain slip is squirted into a plaster mould with a syringe. The eventual leathersoft 'lace' will be strong enough to release gently from the mould soon after the water gloss evaporates. After release, it is returned to the mould to finish drying. Method contributed by Antonella Cimatti. *Photo: Rolando Giovannini.*

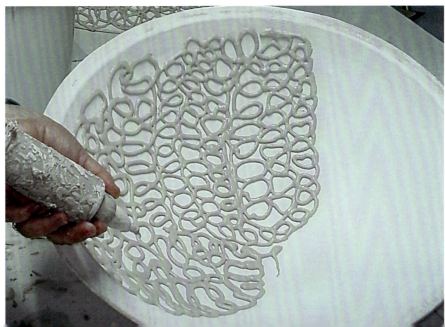

Casting paperclay slip in moulds

Paperclay slip can be poured into, used to take impressions from, and released from a plaster, latex, rubber or sand mould. A plaster mould captures extreme detail from paperclay slip, the same way it does from traditional casting slip, and a latex rubber mould is shown on p. 55. The casting procedure is similar to traditional clay, except that it is possible, and usually better, to release the casting from the mould sooner than if you were using traditional casting slip. Leathersoft paperclay castings are more like fabric and thus not as likely to tear when handled. A few practices carry over from traditional slip-casting: a plaster mould should not be too dry at the start or the first casting of paperclay will stick; and a paperclay casting should be loosened from the plaster while there is still moisture in the paperclay. Thin down paperclay slip with water to find the best consistency for pouring.

For slip-casting, the oatmeal-texture slip recipes in this book will release easily from 'wide mouth' multiple-part moulds, but not so well from 'narrow mouth' designs. If you want to use a plaster mould set with a narrow mouth, open up both halves of the mould and pour or smear thick slip on both sides. After these dry castings have been released, you can join them. There are special formulas for making paperclay pouring slip suitable for narrow-mouth multiple-part moulds, but they are beyond the scope of this book.

Although a direct pouring of paperclay slip into a plaster mould always captures full detail, in a near-life-scale mould it is more difficult to manage a heavy pool of paperclay. The wall thickness tends to thin out high at the edges of the mould. After the casting is dry, thicken a thin or weak rim by joining a new soft coil to it, as shown on p. 33. When feasible, at large-scale it's much quicker to press leathersoft slabs into the mould rather than pour. I wait to mend, trim or cover up any seam lines with paperclay slip and soft paperclay until the entire large casting is dry and at its maximum strength. Dry castings

Susan Schultz (USA), *Unintended Consequences of the Plastic Ocean – Albatross* (detail), 2011. Porcelain paperclay castings have been made to closely resemble trash and debris washed up on the beach. *Photo: Dean Powell.*

hold their shape during trimming and assembly far better than leatherhard, as shown in the chapters ahead.

There are many possibilities for moulds with paperclay. Chapter 4 discusses leathersoft paperclay in press moulds (p. 55). Dry stage paperclay can be a strong enough alternative to plaster for making press moulds (see p. 74, top right).

Slip as release agent

Thin paperclay slip can often be used to keep leathersoft pressings and castings from sticking to glass and other non-porous materials. Brush a thin, nearly transparent layer of paperclay slip over the glass, ceramic glaze or other non-porous surface with a fan brush, or over a non-porous plastic or resin form, and let the coating dry completely before taking an impression. A coating of vegetable spray on non-porous glass or ceramic is another way to keep leathersoft paperclay from sticking.

Brush a thin coat of paperclay slip onto a non-porous surface, like this glass bowl. In five to 15 minutes it will be dry. Thereafter, paperclay pressed softly into the bowl will not stick to it. *Photo: Rosette Gault.*

Turn slip into paperclay

To make modelling paperclay, allow your paperclay slip to thicken in the open air on plaster drying bats or shelves (see pp. 17, 26), as mentioned previously. Here, the process is explained.

The best timing for wedging up your soft paperclay can be determined by a quick visual test. Pour out a layer of thick paperclay slip and keep an eye on it. As soon as the gloss from the water is gone from the top, scrape up the soft paperclay with a flexible rubber rib. Gather the clay into a ball and keep it on hand for a few days, wrapped in plastic or a damp towel. Weather, humidity, air circulation and temperature, the moisture in your plaster, and the thickness and amount poured will all affect the timing of the evaporation process. After a test pour, I know about how thick the pour can be and how long it takes to set up, whether it's five minutes or a couple of hours, and can plan my studio time in rhythm with it. If I want soft paperclay to be ready overnight, I might pour out an extra-thick puddle, for example.

Rosette Gault (USA), *Vision of the Beloved as a Cloud Body*, 2012. Porcelain paperclay, foreground: 37 x 31 x 8 cm (14.5 x 12½ x 3 in.). *Photo: Rosette Gault.*

The slip will set to soft paperclay over a period of five minutes to eight hours depending on the conditions. If conditions are optimal – i.e. paperclay slip is thick, the plaster slab is dry, the plaster itself was properly mixed and cured, the thickness of the plaster slab is deeper than 2–3 cm (¾–1¼ in.), and the weather is dry, paperclay could form very quickly. If the slip is runny, the plaster is wet from multiple pours, no time has been allowed to dry between pours, the plaster is poorly mixed and the weather is humid, the process will take much longer. If the plaster is soaked wet or uncured, the paperclay will not form from slip at all (fresh-made plaster slabs may need as much as a couple of weeks to be dry/cured enough to use for draining water from paperclay slip). If I pour the slip onto a bat or a water-absorbent surface that is not plaster, I would adjust all these factors accordingly to learn the timing.

Usually, I take the easy path and just let time do the job. But when I don't want to wait and I have a smooth plaster surface to pour on, I could make just a small amount of soft paperclay in 2–10 minutes, by a method of 'speed wedging' I have developed. To get a lump started, as seen in the image opposite I will pour or smear a thin puddle over the plaster slab. As soon as the puddle has started to set and the gloss from the water is gone, I scrape ribbons of the soft clay up into a ball.

If I need a larger quantity of soft paperclay quickly, I need a big plaster slab and more slip to pour with. I get a side-to-side rhythm going after I pour. With a large rib, I push most of the wet pool of paperclay slip to the left side of the slab. On the right side, this exposes a thin paperclay layer. To harvest it, I scrape the soft paperclay on the right side up with a soft rib. Next, I repeat the process on the other side. With a rib, I push the top of the remaining pool (on the left) back over the space now available on the right. This procedure exposes a fresh layer of paperclay to harvest on the left. By the time I finish gathering fresh paperclay from the left, fresh paperclay is setting on the right, at the bottom of the pour, ready to harvest again. I repeat this process, side to side, until all the paperclay slip has turned into soft paperclay and been gathered.

Soft paperclay is easy to model and wedge using any traditional method, though it will continue to stiffen as water evaporates. Beyond the leathersoft stage, hand-wedging becomes increasingly difficult. High-pulp paperclay, in the soft state, sets a little quicker than traditional clay, is less plastic and can feel a little like putty. The amount of pulp in the recipe can be a factor in handling, as can the type of base clay.

For more about about lifting off a leathersoft slab, see pp. 45 and 54–5.

Although many factors influence the production of good paperclay, the process is very simple to grasp once it has been tried a few times and you have good paperclay slip to start with. Over recent years, artists have developed countless shortcuts and variations to mixing and preparation methods: experiment.

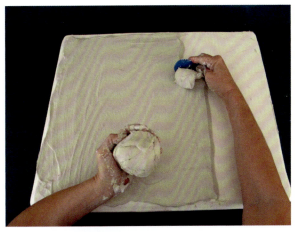

ABOVE LEFT: Pouring freshly-made paperclay slip onto a plaster drying slab. Water will evaporate and soft paperclay will gradually appear. *Photo: Gayle St Luise.*

ABOVE RIGHT: Pour a thick puddle of slip onto a plaster slab. The surface gloss will start to disappear as the excess water drains down into the plaster and evaporates from above. As soon as the gloss is gone, scrape up the very soft layer of fresh paperclay into a ball with a rubber rib. *Photo: Gayle St Luise.*

RIGHT: To test soft wedged paperclay, pull wire though the lump to check that there are no bits of paper fluff visible. Properly-made paperclay looks and feels uniform. If you are hand-building, wedging is optional. If you plan to throw pots on the wheel, wedging is a good idea. *Photo: Melissa Grace Miller.*

The leathersoft state

LEFT: Daniela Schlagenhauf (France), *One of a Kind*, 2010. Porcelain paperclay, width: 50 cm (19¾ in.). Exhibited at Le Lavoir Gallery, Clamart, France, 2011. *Photo: P. Soissons.*

BELOW LEFT: Lift a freshly-poured slab when it is still very soft to get a layer of air underneath. *Photo: Gayle St Luise.*

BELOW RIGHT: Ultra-thin porcelain cup in progress. Leathersoft paperclay can be set on edge and formed in a ring for the sides of a cup. Let this ring dry undisturbed in the open air. Once dry, the walls will not deform and a fresh leathersoft base can be added, which will dry intact. *Photo: Gayle St Luise.*

Familiar ceramic practices such as pinching, coiling and slab-building can all be used with paperclay. Soft modelling paperclay ranges from near-paste consistencies to a state so different from traditional clay that it almost needs a new word to distinguish it. The leathersoft stage is just different enough from the same stage in traditional clay to allow even more variation in the artist's repertoire.

'Leathersoft' is the intermediate moisture state between soft and stiff, when paperclay feels a little like soft leather or wet fabric. A sheet will stay intact when lifted up in the air, or can be rolled in tubes, without surface cracks appearing. Unlike a soft slab in traditional clay, leathersoft paperclay can withstand more handling, lifting and curling stress.

Those who require precision will soon discover that handling paperclay during the 'impressionable' wet stages will influence the dry and fired result. Warping and movement of the form is an example of a typical problem in traditional clay. Ways to prevent or control this warping in paperclay will be covered in this chapter. Best practice at this stage can have an impact on all the steps ahead.

Description of leathersoft paperclay

A leathersoft paperclay slab can be floppy like a wet towel while at the same time being strong enough to roll into tubes, folds or drapes. At first, the sheet will be soft enough to allow you to make a few changes of mind. However, like metal, a leathersoft slab or coil will fatigue and tend to break open where it has been overworked.

Honour Freeman (Australia),
Shape of a Day, 2005. Slip-
cast, hand-built porcelain
paperclay, cotton thread,
height: 45 cm (17¾ in.).
Photo: Michael Kluvanek.

Long coils of leathersoft paperclay will resemble heavy string to lift and arrange. At first they will be too floppy to hold their shape, but soft coils can be interwoven or braided as in basketry or weaving (see p. 11). As leathersoft coils or slabs stiffen (within a half-hour or so, depending on the weather) they can be set to arch in mid-air.

Beyond the leathersoft stage, paperclay stiffens to the point where small surface cracks and texture from the process of folding, stretching and bending start to show, giving a leather- or skin-like appearance. Although surface cracks can sometimes be sprayed lightly with water to re-soften them, it may well be practical to wait until the desired shape itself is completely dry to fill in cracks (see p. 25) or work the surface, as will be discussed in the next chapter.

A folded slab or cut-out can be a stand-alone form. It can be set aside to stand upright and assembled later when it is dry.

Making slabs at leathersoft

There are several ways to prepare thin or thick paperclay slabs with simple tools. We just saw how to start them quickly, by pouring a pool of paperclay slip over a plaster slab (pp. 41–3). Alternatively, if you have a lump of wedged paperclay to hand, you can gather up a soft ball and flatten it with the palm of your hand on a countertop surface to get a 'patty' started. Flip the patty often to keep the top and bottom even and flat. Another easy starting method is to cut a 2–5 cm (¾–2 in.) flat slice from soft paperclay with thin string or wire stretched taut between both hands. A clean, dry rolling pin can be used in the traditional way also. Beginners might roll gently over the paperclay slice or patty, placed between a set of wooden guide rails that stop the rolling pin from thinning the slab more than is wanted. Leathersoft paperclay is strong enough to lift, flip over and move to a nearby dry spot on the table between passes.

Extremely thin sheets can be made and handled with confidence by making sure the table or plaster surface underneath does not get wet and sticky. It may take a few tries to get the knack of lifting and handling thin slabs. If thin slabs start sticking, pry up an edge with a rubber rib. A canvas work surface is not always best for paperclay slabs; imprints of texture from the canvas will have to be smoothed over later. If working with thin slabs on smooth, very dry plaster, sometimes it helps to moisten the plaster with a damp sponge first. The right moisture for your size of slab takes just a little practice if you intend to master this with very thin paperclay porcelain.

Most skills for leathersoft slab construction carry over from traditional clay practice. The first skill is to recognise the easiest time and moisture state at which to handle, cut, curve, fold and drape a leathersoft slab or coil. This will vary depending on your particular paperclay and tools. For those who create slabs from paperclay slip on a plaster work surface, there will be an optimum window of time in which to lift a leathersoft slab up from the plaster (see p. 45). For a freshly-poured slab, it will be in a leathersoft state. Allow a little more time on the plaster than for wedging, before lifting and handling to get the optimum leathersoft stage for smooth folds, curves, drapes and ruffles. The longer you wait, the stiffer the paperclay gets, until the slab can even hold an arch in mid-air (p. 94). The time can range from a few minutes to overnight; on average, it's about 10 minutes to an hour. Artists who want completely flat paperclay slabs will find special instructions about these on p. 54.

Skilled handling at the leathersoft stage is key to success when making larger panels, tiles or flat slabs. The phenomenon of paperclay memory is one of the main causes of unintended warping of slabs and coils during firing. Advanced or professional artists who require this level of control will find more about this just ahead (pp. 49–51).

This leathersoft textured slab was pulled from the mould, then flipped over without tearing. Here, it is draped over the arch of a curved wooden frame to dry in the open air. Plaster mould in foreground. John Grade (artist), assisted by Diane Baxter, Tim Baxter, Travis Stanley and Eddy Radar. John Grade's large project was accomplished with support from Pottery Northwest in Seattle, and finished works were exhibited in New York, 2010. *Photo: Rosette Gault.*

LEFT: Get a crisp edge on a thin leathersoft slab with scissors. Another option is to make cuts all the way, or part-way, through leathersoft paperclay by scribing or slicing with a sharp wooden stick, needle or blade. Trim can be snapped off after it dries. Betsy Nield (South Africa), work in progress. *Photo: Emilyn Nield.*

CENTRE AND RIGHT: Lacy leathersoft cut-outs will be strong enough to lift up and drape. To keep edges crisp, it will often be more practical to wipe cut-lines down after they are dry. As will be explained in the next chapter, wait until the leathersoft cut-out drape dries in place before attaching. *Photo: Gayle St Luise.*

Cut-outs and edges

Leathersoft cut-outs or edges can be easily cut and bevelled with a needle, pointed stick or blade. Sharp edges can sometimes be smoothed down by tracing along the cut line with a finger while the leathersoft cut-out is still flat on the work surface. This is a good moisture state in which to create fluted edges and ruffles, and to perfect soft bevelled edges and corners of a slab or coil. Once the edges are prepared, you can fold or drape the soft slab in position to dry. To trim the final edge, wipe down edges gently after they are dry, at least once, with a damp sponge. If you overwork edges when they are leathersoft, fingerprints and dents will show right away. More trimming methods for dry paperclay cut-outs are described on p. 59, and alternative ways to tuck, roll and trim leathersoft edges are described on p. 73.

Handling delicate cut-outs

A thin cut-out of a lacy shape will be strong enough to handle at the leathersoft stage and to drape over a dry form. As seen in the photo above right, for transit of delicate work it can be helpful to gently tack vulnerable joins and touch-points of the cut-out together by temporarily covering them with little tack-in-place balls of leathersoft paperclay. Later, at the dry stage, it will be easy to pry the little balls up without disturbing the cut-out below. If stress cracks appear, they can be touched up with paperclay slip at the dry stage also.

At this point, my intent is to gently arrange the leathersoft 'drape' of the cut-out in the graceful curve and shape I want to see on the form. As it dries, the most it could shrink by is 10%. I lift the rigid dry lace up from the form where it has dried in place, and put a few soft clay wads between it and the dry torso. I rest it back down on the soft wads and settle the position of the dry lace precisely. When it's just right, I fix and

Altering texture on a leathersoft casting. John Grade presses down sections of thick texture so the surface of each panel is different, but drapes fresh castings over special forms so they can be fitted together later on a big frame. Finished works exhibited in New York, 2010. *Photo: Rosette Gault.*

attach the drape permanently with a wet-dry join using paperclay slip, using a putty or a ball of soft paperclay between the dry parts if needed. Joins at the dry stage are covered in the next chapter (pp. 60–3).

Leathersoft paperclay: two kinds of memory

Wet clay records impressions of events that occur during handling. Whether the clay dries and fires flat or not, or warps as it dries and fires, can be precisely controlled by the artist who takes the time to understand the principles involved. In leathersoft paperclay, our touch influences the mechanics not just of clay particles, but shifts the dynamic interior structure of the cellulose fibre too.

Clay memory, as potters well know, depends on the alignment and distribution of clay particles inside the wet clay. Clay memory can cause dry, wheel-thrown teapot spouts to bend off-centre in the kiln, so potters compensate for this by handling them in a special way when leathersoft, and one of the purposes of wedging clay is to orient all the clay particles in a uniform direction. Paper memory contributes a new dimension to this equation. It is caused by the interior orientation of tiny, coiled tubes that make up the molecular structure of cellulose fibre (p. 24). For this reason, paper and ribbon can hold or remember a curl.

In leathersoft paperclay, clay and paper memory complement each other. Impressions are recorded not just on the surface, but in the interior network of spiral structures in cellulose fibre. Due to this, paperclay can feel just slightly springy at times compared to traditional clay.

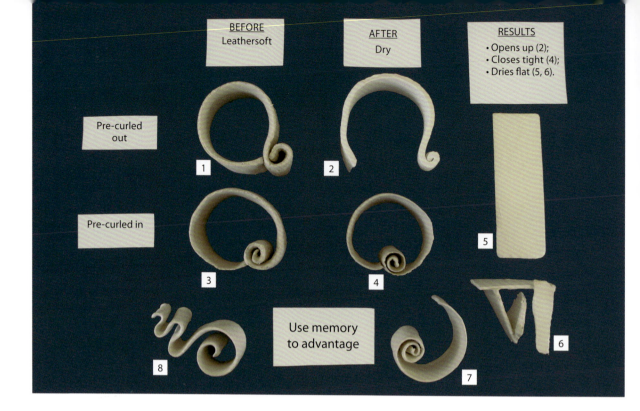

BEFORE
Leathersoft

AFTER
Dry

RESULTS
• Opens up (2);
• Closes tight (4);
• Dries flat (5, 6).

Pre-curled out

Pre-curled in

Use memory to advantage

Controlling paperclay movement: a study

I set up an experiment to demonstrate how to use paperclay memory to advantage when handling a leathersoft slab, to control warping, curling or flatness of paperclay so that it dries and fires as intended. The leathersoft state is an optimum time at which to create a curl that will influence the dry or fired result.

Take a look at the photo above, which shows the results of my experiment. When I started, Examples 1–4 looked like Example 5 – I cut ribbon-like strips of equal size from a single leathersoft slab. I rolled Examples 1, 2, 3, 4, 7 and 8 into very tight curls. Example 5 I placed flat on a plaster surface to dry undisturbed. When the curled strips were still leathersoft, I unwound each one. To make a ring, I placed each on end so that the diameter at the touch point was the same. No paperclay slip was used to make any joins so the clay could move as it dried.

In the first row, the leathersoft curl is Example 1 and the dry is Example 2. In the second row, Example 3 is the leathersoft and Example 4 is the dry. Dry paperclay is dormant and will see little change, but leathersoft or hard paperclay is relatively 'awake' and dynamic.

In Example 2, the seam opened many inches wider from where it started in Example 1. In Example 4, the seam not only stayed closed, it tightened further shut (I call this the Intentional Clamshell Effect). The only difference was the way I intitially handled and precurled the leathersoft examples. In the top row examples, I unwound the tight curl and rewound it tightly in the opposite direction, but in the bottom row examples, I just unwound. As all samples looked the same at leathersoft, I left a little curl

Paperclay memory: Rolled-up leathersoft paperclay, like paper, will curl open (Example 2), curl closed (Example 4) or remain flat (Example 5) as it dries. A direction that is encouraged early on in the wet stages is likely to continue in the stress of a high-temperature firing. Curl the slabs or coils in the direction you want before they set and dry. Some unwind dramatically (Example 2), others curl and tighten in more, according to the direction they 'remember' from earlier handling (Example 4). If uncurled leathersoft strips dry flat they can be cut and joined (Example 6) and will stay flat through the firing, too, if fired right. Otherwise they will warp, a bit like wood can do.
Photo: Gayle St Luise.

as a visual memo. In Example 7, a tightly wound curl opened up to a spiral. Example 8 was a free-form ribbon that stayed where I wanted it.

In practice, this experiment shows that the advanced paperclay artist, who would like seams to snap tight and never come open in drying or firing, can get precise control by pre-handling a leathersoft slab in particular ways before making joins. With some practice, an artist can likewise handle leathersoft slabs to get them to move apart, or to stay completely flat and still.

The shrink-wrap effect

The limit for natural shrinkage from soft to dry is below 10% in most paperclays. Knowing this, avoid wrapping or stretching a leathersoft slab too tightly over a dry part. If draping a soft slab over a dry structure, wait for the leathersoft drape to dry before joining it to the original dry form. Just because you *can* attach soft leathersoft to dry does not always mean you *should*. It is more efficient, and the effect is more fresh and natural-looking, to just let the drape dry naturally, before joining it to the first dry form with slip and leathersoft wads. Patience is rewarded, as shrink-wrap cracking is unlikely if the soft slab shrinks naturally before the join is made.

Drape a leathersoft 'skin' over a dry paperclay structure then tear or trim the edges as you like – to prevent stress cracks in the leathersoft, avoid wrap-arounds or tucking under. As it dries, the soft slab will shrink and tighten over the dry form. When it is dry, use paperclay slip and soft wads of leathersoft paperclay to join the wrap to the dry form below. *Photo: Gayle St Luise.*

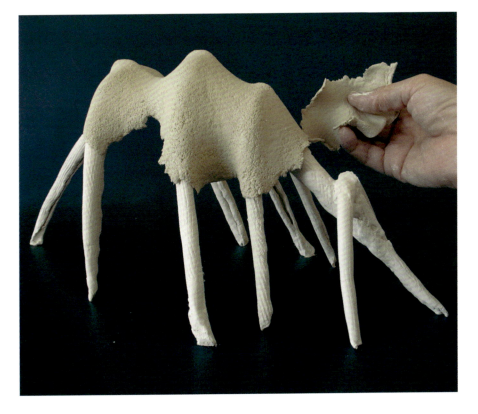

Draped slabs

Draped leathersoft paperclay slabs will not hang right unless the form underneath is in realistic proportion. In the image below left, the surface of the soft slab drape shows a surprising amount of contour detail from ridges in my hand and fingers. Leathersoft slabs imprinted with complex textures or relief can be flipped over, transferred and used for drapes and ruffles, as shown below and on pp. 47 and 49. It helps to attend to smoothing or imprinting texture on leathersoft slabs before draping them.

Handle flowing leathersoft folds only when absolutely necessary. Leaving them to dry untouched allows the curves to fall more naturally and for any shrinkage to be complete. Position the leathersoft drape, then wait for it to dry in place before attaching dry parts. More information on joins involving dry paperclay sections can be seen on pp. 60–3 and in almost every chapter ahead. Cracking is unlikely once you have come to understand both the leathersoft and dry stage properties of paperclays.

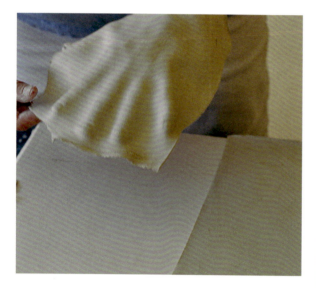

ABOVE: Tap the form (in this case my hand) underneath a leathersoft drape several times on a table to help 'settle' it over the contours of the form, rather than trying to press too hard directly from above. Leathersoft paperclay is vulnerable to fingerprints, so keep any handling to a minimum once the slab looks right. Wait until it sets to leatherhard, or better still dries all the way, before handling. *Photo: Melissa Grace Miller.*

RIGHT: Ribbons of leathersoft paperclay set over a tailor's form can be dry in just hours in the open air and sun. Large draped slabs like these are better joined after they dry. Work in progress by author. *Photo: Rosette Gault.*

Anima Roos (Belgium), *Les Lignes de la Vie 3* (*Lifelines*), 2010. The series ranges in size from 40 x 40 x 5 cm (15¾ x 15¾ x 2 in.) to 40 x 18 x 12 cm (15¾ x 7 x 4¾ in.). *Photo: Anima Roos.*

Big cut-out shapes

Borrowing skills and terms from sewing and tailoring, such as pleats, folds, tucks or darts, I sometimes cut out flat pattern shapes in leathersoft paperclay with a tab-key or arrow dart, or make other markings to match and align between two or more cut-out slabs. Since thick can be next to thin with paperclay, I might cut soft slabs with an extra flap or tab of 2–5 cm (¾–2 in.) at the edge, to roll or fold over (see p. 73). This gives a tidy border, which can be two or three times thicker than the cut-out itself. When the whole slab or cut-out is folded or draped into three-dimensional forms, the thicker border can lend structural support for later assembly, trimming or alteration at the dry stage.

Nest and arrange large leathersoft slabs, ribbons, skirts, robes, sleeves, cuffs or folds together, overlapping and naturally draped. Wait until these drapes are dry to trim edges and join individual pieces together. Those who plan a large-scale project involving paperclay slabs can find ideas for fast and stable practices to assemble and join in stages in the chapters ahead.

Printing, colour and texture in leathersoft

Paperclay artists may, if they desire, treat slabs as if they are fabric or paper, imprinting texture and/or applying surface colour on the leathersoft slab before cutting, folding, stretching or draping. The seams and join can appear quite natural. Under-layers of surface texture or engobes and colour could be started at leathersoft and then worked at every stage up to the final glaze and finish, but those using traditional methods may wait until later stages to apply ceramic decals. Review more ideas and shortcuts for surface treatment and finishing in Chapter 10 (pp. 113–4).

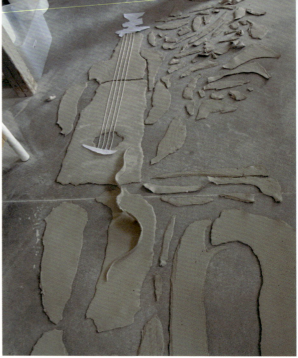

Making big, flat panels

The successful production of big, flat slabs begins with the sequence of handling and drying them at the vulnerable leathersoft stage. Those who start with a lump or slice of soft wedged paperclay, using a rolling pin or slab roller, should review the explanation on pp. 46–7. The key is to create, lift and place them when very soft upon a flat, porous or semi-porous surface such as plaster or dry cement to firm up. They should not be disturbed until fully dry. As discussed on p. 50–1, if you make a curve or bend to thin leathersoft paperclay in one direction, it will 'remember' the movement. Leathersoft clay is often soft enough that it is possible to 'undo' the memory by bending the soft slab in the reverse direction (see also p. 151).

It can be more efficient to skip the wedging and start paperclay slabs within moments of mixing your paperclay slip (see pp. 41–3). A big plaster slab is a simple way to create sheets of an even thickness. On plaster, in the open air, large slabs dry evenly from below and above. Weather, air humidity and circulation, as well as temperature and the moisture condition of the plaster slab you start with, will affect the timing of this process.

The best time to lift a freshly-poured slab off a plaster or tabletop surface occurs just after the soft stage. If you lift it too soon, it will tear and stick, but when the moisture level is right, it releases quite easily. Allow water to soak down and evaporate from above until the paperclay sheet has turned to the leathersoft state. At this point even large sheets will be strong enough to lift up in one piece with your bare hands.

To test if the sheet is ready to release from the work surface, slide the edge of a rubber rib or spatula just under the edge of the slab to loosen a corner, then gently lift it up, about a centimetre or two (these tools are shown in the foreground of the photo on p. 45). Try to minimise the curl at the corner when you do this. At a pre-leathersoft stage the test edge is usually too soft and too floppy to be affected by a minor disturbance at

ABOVE LEFT: Scribe a design all the way through the leathersoft slab to the supporting bowl underneath. Wait until this completely dries and it will be easy to lift and trim (see more about this bowl after it dries on p. 59). *Photo: Gayle St Luise.*

ABOVE RIGHT: Layout of flat paperclay collage, by the author. Transfer fresh large leathersoft slabs to a dry, absorbent surface. Thereafter, slide them sideways if you want, but otherwise do not handle them. When bone-dry, they can be worked and handled safely. If they dry flat, they are likely to remain flat. *Photo: Rosette Gault.*

an edge, but once it is leathersoft, you need to be careful. Ideally, lift this fresh sheet up in one piece from the plaster slab as soon as the plaster allows.

Lift the new soft slab gently, once, to get a microscopic layer of air underneath it; it may feel like a very thick, damp, paper towel. Then lay the slab down flat again on the plaster or on the absorbent surface to dry completely. If it is a big slab it will shrink a little as is dries. There is no need to cover it.

After the first release, provided you leave this slab flat, you are free to begin the process of working the surface textures and colours, and even to add new layers of slip over the top if inspiration strikes. Pre-score your cutting or border lines, if desired, with a sharp stick and straight edge; later, when the slab is dry and flat, you will be able to break the slab apart along these lines (p. 67). Avoid the temptation to handle or move your new panel or flat sheet until it is dry. If the leathersoft slab is allowed to dry flat and undisturbed, it usually stays that way through firing.

Press soft paperclay into moulds

You can press soft and leathersoft paperclay into moulds of all kinds (see also pp. 40–1). With press moulds, use the softest wedged paperclay for full surface detail. Stiffer paperclay will only give the basic contour of the mould, not the surface detail.

After soft paperclay has dried, fill in any seam lines or stray marks with paperclay slip. Trim by fettling or carving down with a blade, as shown in the next chapter. Press castings take less time to release from a large mould than a direct pour of paperclay slip and the walls will be more even. Leathersoft castings can be pulled out or released from a plaster mould sooner than pressings made with traditional clay. Just after the press, it sometimes helps to model an extra tab at the edge of the casting, which you can gently pull on to help release the pressing from the mould. You can trim this off after it has served its purpose.

With latex rubber moulds (see left), one can either press soft paperclay, or pour thick paperclay slip or paste in or over them. If you are casting in a rubber mould with undercuts, let the paperclay casting dry inside the latex so that the form does not distort when you peel the mould away.

Most release agents for mixed media sculpture casting are compatible with paperclay, but a thin coating of paperclay slip on a bowl 'mould' will also keep leathersoft coils or slabs from sticking to the glass or non-porous surface, as we saw on p. 41. You can also press soft paperclay over cast resins, vinyl, polyurethane, fibreglass or plastics to get an imprint. Wait until the pressing turns leatherhard to release it naturally. Later, a dry paperclay pressing can both give and take impressions, and dry paperclay is tough enough to serve as an alternative to plaster press moulds.

Starting from a single press mould, artists can replicate variations on a theme (see works in progress on p. 86).

BELOW: Use a soft latex mould to quickly duplicate detailed low relief carving. Roll or press the the latex texture over leathersoft paperclay slabs. Imprinted soft paperclay can be folded or rolled into shapes for an alternative to flat tiles. Another method would be to let thick paperclay slip dry completely in a latex mould with undercuts, since dry paperclay will be strong enough to peel the latex mould from. Work in progress, Pamela Bird (USA). *Photo: Anna Oakden.*

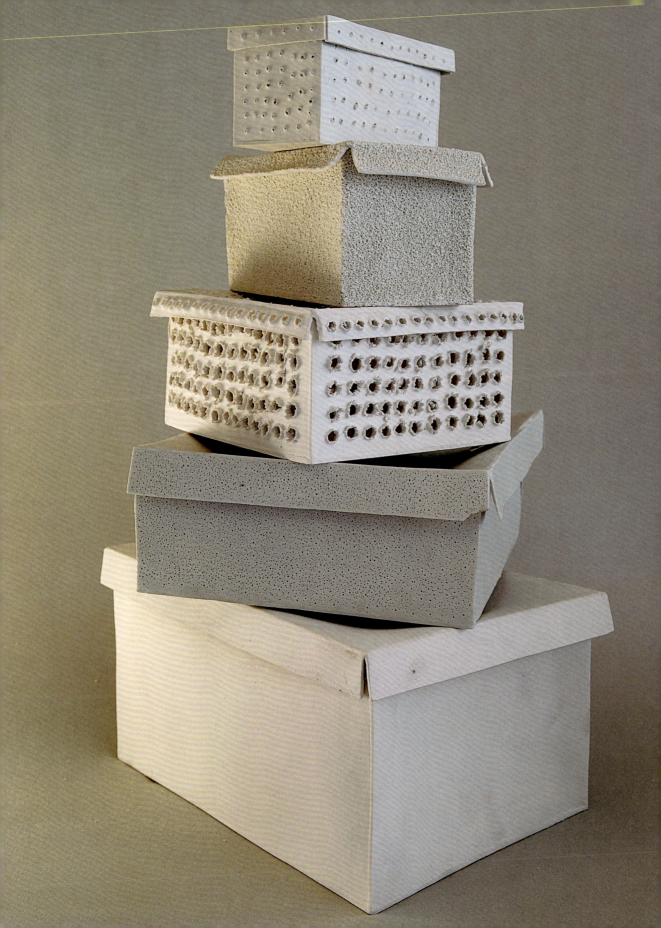

5

The dry state

Dry paperclay

In its bone dry state, paperclay is stable and the risk of cracking or warping has passed. The work will not feel damp or cool. There is also a visual cue, as most paperclays harden to a lighter colour. During the transition from dry to wet, the base clay may shrink between 2 and 10% depending on the recipe, and the paperclay version shrinks only 1% less than the base clay.[1] The tensile strength and hardness of dry paperclay is nearly double that of traditional clay (see p. 151). Dry paperclay is not watertight but keeps for years under shelter or in storage. Like traditional clays, paperclay is best fired when totally dry.

Since dry and wet paperclay combine so easily, dry parts can be assembled, cut, joined, contoured, carved and altered as often as desired. Those who prefer the non-linear approach to making will continue to build at this stage, combining dry and wet paperclay in ways that are not possible with traditional clay.

This is a good time to do clean-up and trimming. Artists who want a hard, rock-like ceramic result that does not slake down in water will finish with ceramic glaze and firing (un-fired finishes are discussed in Chapters 10 and 12).

Paperclay can always be treated as if it is traditional clay. The increase in strength and the opportunity to make repairs at the dry stage may be plenty of change to get used to. If you wish to work in the traditional style, treat dry paperclay as normal and place dry forms in a kiln for the first biscuit firing, before applying glazes and carrying out a second firing. However, the next several chapters show new territory for artists who want to use a non-linear approach. Use as few or as many of the new practices as you require.

About re-wetting when dry

Dry paperclay can be dried and re-wetted as many times as you like until you are ready to finish and/or fire. Deliberately re-wetting a dry section will prepare it for a join, addition, patch, carving, contour, or for new surface texture or colour. Add moisture with a damp sponge, brush or spray by soaking or dipping the dry section briefly in water or paperclay slip, or by wrapping a wet rag or towel 'bandage' over the area for a short while. If necessary, thin, dry sections can be softened up enough to be bent or moved.

Moisture will evaporate from the dry paperclay surface quickly. You'll see the part or edge that you are working on absorb water while sections near or below it stay dry and hard. After the first few tries, you will be able to see and feel the best amount of moisture and timing for your particular paperclay. Also note that, with persistent re-

LEFT: Einat Cohen (Israel), *Boxes*, 2006. Porcelain paperclay, height: 90 cm (35½ in.). *Photo: Einat Cohen.*

LEFT: Maria Oriza (Spain), *Dos Hitos*, 2010. Stoneware paperclay with iron cobalt and manganese oxides, 54 x 10 x 77 cm (21¼ x 4 x 30¼ in.) and 59 x 10 x 81 cm (23¼ x 4 x 32 in.). *Photo: Maria Oriza.*

RIGHT: Robyn Becker (Australia), set of porcelain figures, 2010. Thin cut-out shapes can be laid flat to dry. Secure both sides 'dry to dry' with paperclay slip along the seam. Height of tallest form: 12¾ cm (5 in.). *Photo: Robyn Becker.*

wetting, paperclay will eventually get waterlogged. How long this will take depends on how thick the walls are; thin walls can start to soften in five minutes, while thicker walls take half an hour or more. If small areas soften more than you want, the remedy is simple: dry them hard again. Note also that dry paperclay, when submerged in water, will start to slake down.

Assemble, press or contour soft layers of paperclay over rigid dry parts. If rewetting of the dry part has been underway for a time, the part underneath might start to soften in thin or unsupported areas. When this happens, stop. Resume work later when the structure returns to the high tensile strength of the dry state.

Because of its absorbency, a matt, dry, paperclay surface readily accepts wet surface coatings and multiple layerings of paperclay slip, as well as engobes, glazes and a variety of textures and finishes. Single-fire glaze is best applied to dry paperclay that is at maximum dryness, absorbency and pre-firing strength. Glazing and firing will be discussed at length in Chapters 10 and 11.

Benefits of fast drying

Wet paperclay can be dried near a warm kiln, a fan, a heater or even in direct sunlight. It may help to turn the work periodically. Large works can be force-dried for a few hours in the kiln at very low settings or with a door open, as long as the temperature of the paperclay stays below the boiling point of water (99.98°C/212°F).

TOP RIGHT: Edges and rims on dry ware can be softened with a damp sponge. If thin sections start to soften too much, let them dry again. *Photo: Gayle St Luise.*

BOTTOM RIGHT: We saw this bowl on p. 54. To make a new border for a dry bowl, fit a fresh leathersoft coil along the outside of the dry rim. When the coil dries, use a layer of thick paperclay slip for a quick and secure adhesive between dry parts. The new, dry coil rim will not deform or get fingerprints. *Photo: Gayle St Luise.*

Leave work in progress uncovered to dry between sessions. Any new layer of moisture introduced during a work period is unlikely to penetrate all the way through the dry paperclay. You can intentionally dry your paperclay between sessions. This process saves time and is practical for several reasons.

As the paperclay alternates between wet and dry stages, the form slowly contracts and expands. Joins that survive this gentle expansion and contraction before firing tend to do well in the kiln also. The fast drying process makes potentially weak areas obvious; cracks will show the precise areas where repairs or special reinforcement could be needed in advance of firing. Cracks tend not to be a problem with a well-made paperclay recipe, but we will discuss dry stage repairs and reinforcements later in this chapter (pp. 63–4).

When you have finished making adjustments to the dry paperclay, your project will be dry enough to fire within hours or days. With this new method of fast drying, there will be little doubt that the interior, thick sections of your work are dry enough to fire. Traditionalists who would rather keep paperclay wrapped up wet until all the assembly and trimming process is complete may need to allow weeks or months for the inside of some forms to dry completely, even in the open air, and several months if the work is kept covered to dry very slowly. For works using the linear method of assembly, open-air or fast drying will be more successful if the walls are even. Use caution if a slow-dried work has many thick or thin joints, as it is at risk of drying unevenly or warping. In paperclay, stress cracks can always be repaired afterwards. Those who use the new method of assembly with stable, dry parts and fast drying between sessions need not be concerned over this.

Transporting a dry paperclay panel to the kiln with a hoist. Work in progress, Paul Chaleff (USA). *Photo: Paul Chaleff.*

About bonds and joins

Though it is possible to make secure joins between two leatherhard paperclay parts, as in traditional methods, the bond will take more time to dry and set, in part because there is no moisture difference between two leatherhard sides. Many artists find that dry-dry or dry-wet joins will set more quickly. Wet cellulose fibres in paperclay slip stiffen up quickly on contact with dry paperclay, resulting in a tight grip between the parts (see p. 147).

For making a join between dry pieces of paperclay, where the join will be weight-bearing, the general rule is the same as for making joins at the leatherhard stage in traditional ceramics. Moisten the sides that will be joined together with water and paperclay slip, scratch texture at the points of intended contact, and press the wet, sticky ends together (see p. 62). The moisture of the slip will soak into the dry sections in minutes, holding the parts together. The bond will continue to set until entirely dry.

When a join will not be weight-bearing and is decorative, attach a dry or wet part to the dry paperclay, without scoring, with a generous dab of paperclay slip. The paperclay slip hardens in place quickly and the excess can be trimmed with a sponge or fettle blade. In Chapter 3 (p. 31), we saw how a coating of paperclay slip can fill gaps and seal between dry coils or interwoven strips of paperclay, so scoring between them is optional.

The majority of joins between dry parts will be as strong or stronger than those made at leatherhard. Indeed, fresh, wet bonds between dry sections will set and tighten as the assembly dries. Each wet-to-dry addition will reinforce a join.

ABOVE LEFT: Visible dry strength during dry slab construction. Dry paperclay joins can be observed before firing and reinforced if necessary. Work in progress, Paul Chaleff (USA). *Photo: Paul Chaleff.*

ABOVE RIGHT: Because of the extreme moisture difference, moisture has soaked up these dry legs a considerable distance from the point of contact, a pool of thick paperclay slip at the base. The next day the sculpture and legs were dry. A dab of paperclay slip over dry paperclay sets in moments because of this effect. The process is easy to see in action, because wet clay is a darker colour than dry. High-pulp Limoges porcelain paperclay, work in progress by the author. *Photo: Rosette Gault.*

LEFT AND RIGHT: This set of dry porcelain curls was made by extrusion. These are being assembled when dry and at maximum strength. In the right-hand picture, the three dry curls have been joined. Seam lines have been smoothed over and wiped down with a damp sponge. The rewetted areas will dry between work periods. Collaboration in progress by author and Colleen Mettler. *Photo: Rosette Gault.*

Types of joins with dry paperclay

Variations of joins that can be made on dry paperclay range from simple to complex depending on the size and scale of the project and the imagination of the artist. Artists using the non-linear approach will integrate and combine the paperclay in all its moisture states, using skills from the earlier chapters.

The simplest join is to add a wet extension to a dry part. An example might be adding a freshly-modelled leaf to the end of a 'vine', dry coil or rolled tube. To do this, you would re-wet the area on the vine where the wet piece will be joined, add paperclay slip, rough up the same area on the vine and press the soft paperclay leaves there. You can contour and model the new leaf out from the dry vine. Another form of wet-dry join is thickening or adding contour over a dry part. Re-wet the dry part, score the area, and apply some paperclay slip. Press, model and contour the softened paperclay surface as part of the join. An example might be building up muscles on a dry stick figure.

With a dry-to-dry join, spot areas on both sides will need to be rewetted with paperclay slip and often some soft paperclay will be helpful to add in the seam. Some artists like to force wet areas of new joins dry with a heat gun, but this tends to dry only the exterior of thick joins. You can't assume that a really thick join is fully dry until the interior has had time to dry. This may take several hours or overnight depending on the climate.

With very large-scale pieces, complex joins can be done in short stages. I have developed a method of tacking and joining large, dry parts together by placing soft, fresh balls of paperclay at regular intervals along the seam, which serve as soft links or bumpers between the two sides. These allow me to align and adjust both dry parts with precision. In a very short time, these balls will be dry and hard. At this point, I check that the assembly has dried in balance also. If I want to make adjustments, it is simpler to pry the links apart to replace a ball or two than to pull apart a whole seam. After the central linked assembly is completely dry, secure and stable, I fill the gaps in the seam between and over the hardened clay links with fresh, soft paperclay. I call this the 'point wad' method. Very large, dry shapes can be assembled

To prepare a join, re-wet the dry areas to be joined and apply paperclay slip to them. If the join will be weight-bearing, score texture on both surfaces. I often place a point wad of soft paperclay between the two parts, then press gently and adjust the hard and dry parts at the angle I want. The wet sections will dry in a few hours. *Photo: Gayle St Luise.*

For a weight-bearing join, prepare both surfaces at the joining point by rewetting, scoring and adding paperclay slip to each end. Press the soft new handle firmly in place. Trim the excess paperclay slip with a damp sponge if need be. To test the join, wait until all is dry. *Photo: Gayle St Luise.*

ABOVE LEFT: Join big, dry works in stages. First tack soft point wads at waist, neck, base, etc., on dry shells. Score, add slip, then press together. *Photo: Rolando Giovannini.*

ABOVE RIGHT: To repair a vulnerable weight-bearing section, adapt the kinds of joins used in carpentry, such as the post and lintel or bevel and mitre. Advanced joins like these are best done in stages. Build a fresh 'post' on one side and let it dry. Meanwhile, open a loose fitting hole for this post on the other side. Join the sections quickly and neatly with paperclay slip when both are dry. Work in progress, the author. *Photo: Gayle St Luise.*

securely to dry paperclay armatures or structures by this method, too, as will be discussed in Chapter 8.

Repairs and reinforcement

Inspect all your dry work, especially any weight-bearing joins, for signs of weakness such as cracks, loose joins or very thin areas. A repair or reinforcement process is beneficial at this stage, because firing will expose any weakness that had not been attended to. Properly mixed and joined paperclay rarely needs repair or extra care when it's dry, but not everyone has a good paperclay to start with, due to misinformation, inexperience or other factors beyond immediate control.

To make repairs, adapt the skills described for joins in this chapter (also pp. 25, 31–2). Paperclay artists using the non-linear approach will usually wait to patch or reinforce thin or vulnerable areas until the thin sections are dry, and therefore at their maximum possible tensile strength and stability. It would not be possible to make repairs or reinforcements like this at the dry stage of traditional ceramic.

Until you build up some experience with paperclay joins, it will help to test them before you fire. To test, gently apply pressure to the join when it is dry to see if it holds firm. If the join fails, add a little more paperclay slip in the seam and allow it to dry (often beginners are too timid with moisture and don't intially use enough paperclay). Evaluate whether it is faster to just re-do the join; it may be quicker, depending on the type of paperclay you have in your mix, as well as the location and purpose of your join. Another way to test your new repair or patch is by fast or open-air drying it, as described earlier in the chapter. Each time you make a secure, dry join, you learn how much rewetting, scoring, paperclay slip and soft paperclay is needed. See images next page.

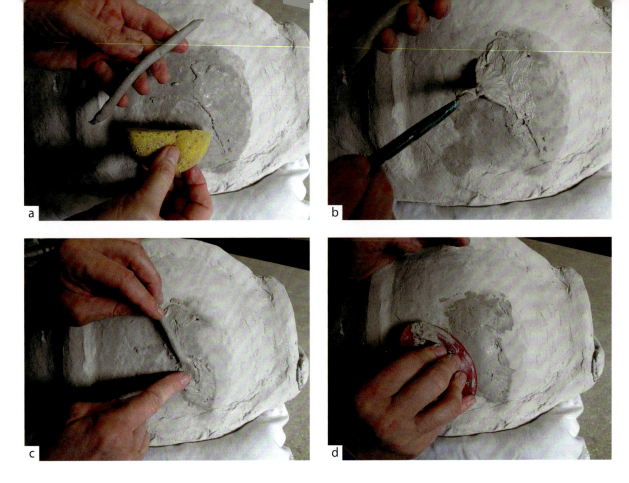

You can do a bisque firing to double-check for cracks or weakness, which will sometimes show up then. Attempts to repair clean breaks in bisque, and sometimes even dry paperclay, will take practice. Scratching and roughing up the surfaces to be joined will create more surface area for the paperclay slip to seep in. For a work-around when this is not possible, fettle or carve wider lines at the crack site, fill the open line with paperclay paste or slip (or cover the contour with soft paperclay) and let this shrink in place. There are 'over the counter' adhesives, such as superglues and epoxies, that are used in traditional ceramic, and these work well with paperclay, too. Repairs and joins for bisque-fired work will be further discussed in the next chapter (p. 78). More practices for joining complex structures can be found in Chapters 7 and 8, which explain how paperclay structures and frames are strong enough to serve as armatures.

Trimming edges and surfaces

To soften the contours of sharp or rough dry edges, wipe, dab or even rub a damp sponge along the top of the edges, as shown in the image above. If you rub a dry paperclay surface too hard or too long with a damp sponge, clay particles may be washed out and little bits of lint will start to release. These can be brushed off when the surface dries.

ABOVE: a) Re-wet a wide area around the crack with a damp sponge or brush. Have some soft paperclay ready to patch with. b) Apply paperclay slip in and around the crack. c) Press the soft paperclay into the crack. If need be, re-wet the dry area again. d) Finish by gently smoothing the repair with a rib and wiping down with a damp sponge. Wait until all is completely dry to trim. If paperclay and patch mix was not well-mixed, the crack will probably need another patch. Find more about paperclay slip patch mixtures on p. 25. *Photo: Gayle St Luise.*

Fitting a folded leathersoft slab to the body of a thin, dry teapot, preparing to make a join between them. Moisten dry or leathersoft edges to be joined with paperclay slip, scratch surface texture and then press them together. *Photo: Gayle St Luise.*

When you require more than a sponge to trim an advanced-level dry project, gently scrape across the rough edges, dings or dents with a stainless-steel flexible rib or sharp blade. Some irregular edges may need gentle carving with a fettling knife or a wood rasp tool. If you must use a pottery trimmer, keep the edge as sharp as possible. Pottery trimming tools are better suited for soft paperclay than hard.

To get a crisp, straight line on the dry edge of a flat tile or panel (see p. 106), I use a table edge as a guide. I scrape a line in multiple passes with a metal rib, blade or wood rasp. A rasp works very well on dry, larger works of porcelain and non-grog paperclay, but requires a little practice and a gentle hand.

Should the surface of your project need sanding rather than scraping, a kitchen pot scrubber or ceramic mesh will last much longer than sandpaper. These tools can be cleaned periodically and re-used. To add texture to surfaces that are too smooth, scratch open the surface with a serrated rib or needle tool, just as if it was wet.

Since sanding or scraping dry paperclay creates dust, wipe down edges and work areas periodically with a damp sponge. I place a damp, wet towel just below my work area to catch paperclay dust before it falls on the floor. This simple dust trap is easy to rinse out in water later. Wear a breathing mask and eye protection if you anticipate a dry carving or fettling process will be lengthy.

Dry paperclay can be polished smooth by burnishing and terra sigillata methods. Chapter 10 will explain more options for achieving the desired colour and texture in surfaces.

Trimming for a close fit with other dry parts

Sections and parts that need a close fit can be matched and measured to each other with accuracy when they are dry. Dry sections of scale models, design prototypes and maquettes can be refined, altered and updated as often as you like, without your having to rebuild the entire arrangement and all the parts (see photo next page). Building scale models and maquettes is discussed in Chapter 7 (pp. 81–4).

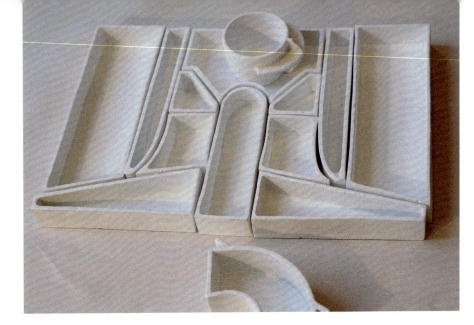

Close fitting a design for nesting trays. The fit between parts can be tested as often as desired at the dry stage, because parts are strong enough to be handled. Sections of the dry model can be altered, removed and replaced until you are satisfied. Work in progress, student of Mariane Thorsen (Denmark), 1996. *Photo: Mariane Thorsen, Denmark Design School.*

Trimming the interior and back side

The inside trim can look as beautiful as the outside because dry paperclay is strong enough to be turned over and modelled from behind. To expose the back of your paperclay, put the dry work front-side down on a layer of soft padding, such as an old blanket, pillow, foam rubber, bubble pack or towel. Using any of the joining methods described in this chapter, fill in gaps, reinforce thin areas, and smooth and cover rough joins on the back side. With a fresh coil or strip of leathersoft paperclay, you may model bridges or hooks on which the work can hang after it is fired, or you can model an opening to fit hardware for hanging, to be glued in later.

When all is dry, test these new weight-bearing joins before firing. Pull them gently with your hand. If they are stable, hang the work on a wall for a few moments, making sure you are ready to catch it if it falls. Mark the spot where the work will hang from a nail and model a pocket around that spot. You can also mark two spots between which to string wire, then build or attach some rings or hooks to thread the wire through later (or just score the marked areas, for application of heavy-duty glue after firing).

Allow plenty of wiggle room in openings designed to receive mounting bolts or screws, or by which the piece will hang. Space for post-firing grout or adhesive may be needed. The diameter of the holes will shrink a little during firing. Holes for hanging should be about 10–25% wider in diameter than you actually need, to leave room around the nail for a layer of silicone gel, museum wax, earthquake or mounting putty.

Cutting dry paperclay for building

In addition to the methods for trimming and finishing, artists cut dry paperclay as part of the building process. Many methods and tools for cutting cardboard, plasterboard, drywall, wood, metal and glass can be adapted for paperclay.

For example, the process for cutting a line in a large, dry slab of paperclay will be familiar. Scribe a straight line on the surface of the dry paperclay, where you want the

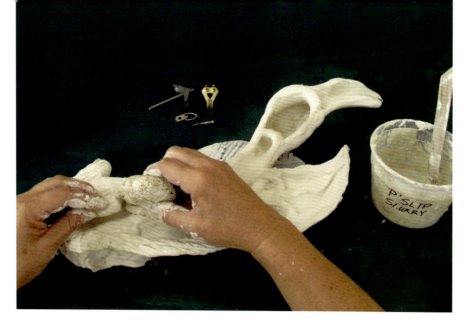

RIGHT: Fitting *Flamingo* for hanging. Model a place for installation hardware to be fitted in the back. I put arched coils in the neck and head to serve as hooks, and little clay hooks in the beak. Reinforce vulnerable areas from behind or below. Smooth over all the joins with paperclay slip. Wipe with a damp sponge to finish, as shown here. *Photo: Gayle St Luise.*

Flat slabs or panels can be scribed on with a sharp blade and then snapped apart like glass or drywall. Here, the edge of a table is used to stabilise the ruler and the dry paperclay slab. A shallow line is draw on the surface (above left). With the table for leverage, one side is pushed down to open and the slab is broken along the line (above right). *Photo: Gayle St Luise.*

break to be, with a needle tool or sharp blade. Place half of the slab on a table with the intended cut line close to the table's edge. Gently and slowly apply pressure to the section that overhangs the table until the dry paperclay breaks apart along the line. Alternatively, you can align the score you have made with the table edge and strike the paperclay on the line in one quick go, the way one can snap open a scribed line in a piece of glass.

Bending and breaking dry paperclay along *curved* lines takes practice. You can break off small sections along a scribed curve a little at a time, going slowly at first, or you may be able to use a jigsaw. Methods for cutting curves from stained glass or mosaic work can be adapted if you pursue this technique.

If you know where your cut lines will be ahead of time, pre-score deep guide lines on the surface of a leathersoft slab with a pointed stick or needle. Make sure you don't quite pierce all the way through. Leave 5–10% of the slab line uncut to discourage the edges from curling or warping until the entire slab dries. If the scored slab dries intact and flat, the sides will snap apart and the line will remain very crisp. Soften any sharp edges with a damp sponge or carving blade when dry.

Sawing paperclay

In some ways, building with dry paperclay is like building with some kinds of soft wood. It is absorbent; it can have grain; it is hard enough to cut, carve or chisel on. Power or hand tools of all sizes and types, including saws, drills, routers, Dremel tools, jigsaws and lasers, can cut leatherhard, dry or fired paperclay. Crisp machine cuts can be done pre- or post-firing. To reduce wear and tear on a saw blade, it can be helpful to pre-score the line at the leathersoft stage (see p. 55). As wet or leatherhard paperclay is softer than dry, some kinds of power tool cuts may be easier to start at that stage, but you do risk the clay moving or warping. There are too many possible projects to give a hard and fast rule, but cuts and assembly with dry paperclay forms tend to be more stable and predictable.

Carving dry paperclay

In addition to trimming and finishing methods using fettling tools, ribs and blades, dry paperclay can be carved and chiselled on quite deeply if desired. Unlike a soft stone, if you carve down too much, it it easy to add more soft paperclay to build up again. Many artists like the fact that spot areas can easily be softened up by draping a wet rag over the area and waiting a little while. Switch back and forth between carving on soft or hard surfaces in the same piece to get the best of both methods. The dry paperclay below will be strong enough to support the soft paperclay added on top.

Thick, dry sections or chunks of paperclay will require cutting tools like a crowbar, a hammer and chisel. Some even need a chainsaw. Use power tools such as drills and saws only if you have learned appropriate safetey procedures. Use eye and breathing protection. It is beyond the scope of this book to describe the adaptations for power tools in any detail except to say that cutting with a power tool normally does not shatter the dry paperclay. Hammering hard with a mallet and sharp chisel on a thick, dry chunk of paperclay will not shatter it either.

When the project is fired, some paperclay base recipes are formulated to harden to the density and hardness of stone or marble (such as porcelain and stoneware varieties). The artist who takes the time to integrate and refine methods here will find many ways to adapt and personalise stone-cutting practices for lightweight, hard and durable paperclay. Carving on fired paperclay is discussed in Chapter 11 (p. 131).

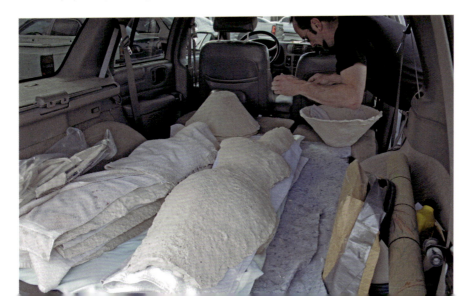

Dry paperclay is stable in transport. Here, two stacks of thin, dry paperclay porcelain parts are en route for assembly from one studio to another. *Photo: Rosette Gault, courtesy Aardvark Clay (USA) with Robert Murphy assisting.*

ABOVE LEFT: Dry or leatherhard paperclay can be worked with power tools, Dremel tools, drills and laser-cutters. *Photo: Gayle St Luise.*

ABOVE RIGHT: Paperclay, as a carving medium, has some advantages over wood, stone or plaster. If you chip too much off or change your mind about any contour, you can built it back up again using wet-on-dry methods. *Photo: Gayle St Luise.*

LEFT: Take full advantage of the strength of dry paperclay. Tack dry shapes in place with soft wads of paperclay and paperclay slip. It's quick to undo or move parts as much as you want. After weight-bearing joins dry, reinforcement layers can be added to thicken weak or thin sections (see p. 94). More about support structures for firing porcelain shell assemblies is discussed on pp. 99–100. *Photo: Rosette Gault.*

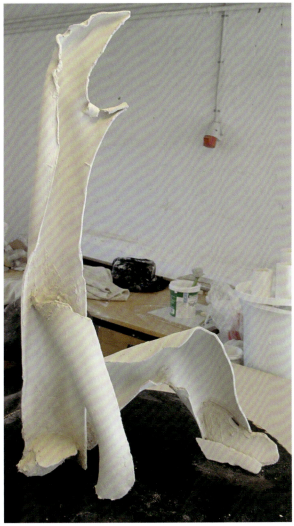

Endnotes

1. See endnote 2, p. 27.

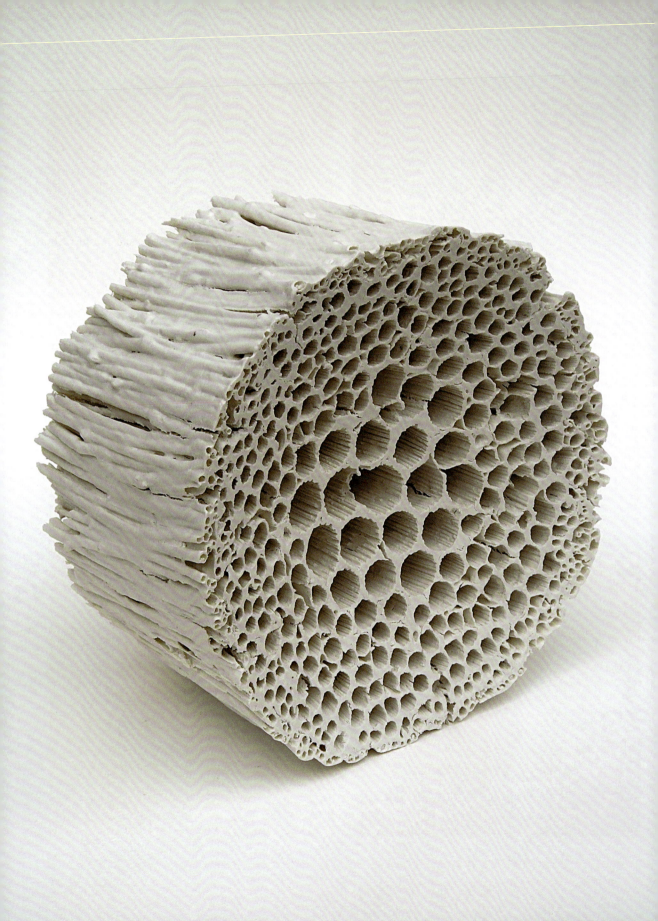

6

Integration of methods

The freedom of new paperclay methods

The fact that, when using paperclay, most choices are reversible and most cracks or accidents can be easily repaired means we can arrive at a final work of art by a personalised sequence of decisions. This might involve multiple layers, wet-to-dry assembly, subtractions and additions to get unique surface effects and forms. This chapter looks at ways to integrate paperclay practices and principles. Earlier chapters have introduced the various moisture states of paperclay and some possibilities of the non-linear approach, as well as examples of how the methods and tools of 'mixed media' have been adopted by paperclay artists, making ceramic practices and clay studios accessible to a wider group of artists.

If so much choice and freedom seems overwhelming, start with small and simple steps and enjoy every moment of the discovery process. Beginners are advised to practise classic pinch or coil methods to get a feel for both wet and dry-state paperclay, and to gain direct experience in the changes in the medium as water evaporates. Like a new friend, your trust in paperclay will grow with experience.

The key principles and new ideas for building with paperclay are:

1. Paperclay elements are dynamic. Paperclay work may be at times both/and/or flexing and curling, hard and soft, stable and inert, shrinking and expanding, water-absorbent and -resistant, strong and weak. Many combinations are possible.

LEFT: Thérèse LeBrun (Belgium), *Structure 31*, 2009. Porcelain paperclay, 17 x 25 cm (6¾ x 10 in.). *Photo: Paul Gruszow.*

RIGHT: Build over a dry paperclay frame with leathersoft slabs. Add or subtract dry or wet parts as desired. Wait for the paperclay frame to dry completely in between work sessions. A dry frame provides more effective support than leatherhard, and it is very stable. Work in progress, Malene Pedersen (Denmark). *Photo: Malene Pedersen.*

Elzbieta Grosseova (Czech Republic) has used layers of leathersoft paperclay rolled with dry ceramic materials and glazes that will fuse in the firing, 2011. *Photo: Elzbieta Grosseova.*

2. It is possible to test and preview the the integrity of a new paperclay construction by fast or open-air drying. Cracks, if detected early, can be helpful messages and shrinkage can be put to practical use. Fresh-made paperclay is often better than 'aged'.

3. The flow of air and moisture through a paperclay form before firing is an advantage that can allows precision control and detail, especially in a complex project.

4. The dry state is more than a last chance to transport finished work into a kiln. At the dry stage, paperclay reaches its maximum possible strength, stability and water absorbency, so it can be trusted as a state to build from and return to often. This offers an alternative sense of timing than that of traditional ceramic.

5. Artists have precise control over the gentle movements of paperclay through all its moisture and fired states. The ebb and flow of moisture has a predictable rhythm.

Examples of integrated methods

In addition to what we have seen earlier, the order of assembly and windows of time in which methods can be carried out will vary. The process can be as simple as using a single drying period or extend to multiple instances of wet-to-dry work.

Here is a brief example of how a non-linear 'return to dry' making process might go. I have a set of dry, carved paperclay stamps. I use them to stamp a pattern in a soft slab of paperclay. I then cut a triangle out of this stamped and textured slab and smooth the edges. I fold this in mid-air to arch it into a tent and *let it dry*. Then, using soft coils, I add longer legs to the edges of the dry tent and *let these dry*. To create socks, I dip the tips of the dry legs in paperclay slip and *let these dry*. Perhaps the next day I don't like the socks. Would boots be better? I sculpt some boots to fit. Do I let them dry before I join them? I could do it either way. There are many ways to arrive at the desired result.

Contemporary paperclay artists are inpsired by methods from media outside ceramics. Some examples of adaptations for paperclay practice follow.

Adapting methods from collage and papermaking

Cut-and-paste practices from paper can be adapted for paperclay. Start with a collage of flat, dry, cut-out or torn strips from paperclay slabs. Transform these into bas relief by adding contours or layerings of soft paperclay. After these parts are dry, carve and trim them before assembly. You could start to work the surface finish at this stage (more on surface treatment and colour will be explained in Chapter 10). Later these dry collage parts will be strong enough to handle, stand upright and integrate into a large form using dry-to-dry or wet-to-dry joins.

Adapting methods from textile art and printmaking

Paperclay practices can be adapted from fashion design, millinery, sewing, weaving and other fibre arts, including folding, pleating, pinning, stretching, draping, making ruffles, and the use of patterns and templates (see p. 54). To get tight joins between seams, advanced artists might take advantage of the controlled warp methods we discussed in Chapter 4 (pp. 50–1). Printmaking methods for colour and surface texture can be incorporated in the building and assembly process, too. These can be combined with casting and mould-making, as we will discuss at the end of the chapter.

When draping and wrapping a folded, delicate or lacy part, sometimes it is better to wait until the part dries, then join between the two strong, dry, delicate parts using soft balls of paperclay (the point wad method, pp. 62–3). Patching, carving and alteration are better attempted at the dry stage also.

A soft slab can be stretched tight over a solid hump and cut to fit. Excess at the edge of the slab can be rolled up like a fabric hem to build some reinforcement at the seam line, without having to add a soft coil. In a hump mould like this, be sure to pull and release the casting from the hump before it is fully dry so it will not shrink and stick. Set the leatherhard 'seam' edges flat on a clean, level surface to complete the process of hardening and drying and minimise the chance of warping. Work in progress by author. *Photo: Gayle St Luise.*

Parts can be assembled and disassembled many times until the fit dries as desired. Here leatherhard and leathersoft drapes are custom-fitted around a dry 'head' that was modelled and carved earlier. In a situation like this, leave a little extra room in the curve of the leathersoft drape to allow for the shrink wrap effect. It may be better to wait until the new drape is dry before joining it to the other dry parts. Work in progress, Larry Thwing (USA). *Photo: Rosette Gault.*

Adrien Miller (USA) drapes a leathersoft slab over one side of a large bisque-fired form to take a impression of the contour. He contours the edges of the leathersoft slab so it releases easily from the face with no undercuts after it dries. When the soft slab dries, it can be used as a press mould. Dry paperclay press moulds are a viable alternative to plaster and can be recycled when the project is completed. *Photo: Rosette Gault.*

Adapting methods of mould-making, casting and imprinting

Use soft paperclay to take impressions of any texture or contour (see p. 55). When hard enough, these can later be used as stamps, or dry paperclay can be carved for stamps also. What is more, dry unfired paperclay is strong and water-absorbent enough to be used for a press mould, which can be recycled when the edition is completed. Paperclay also releases well from plaster, rubber or sand-cast moulds, and slip-cast paperclay is strong enough to be carved.

Adapting new technologies for ceramic design and prototyping

Practices for surface-print transfer, etching, imprinting, CAD/CAM modelling, rapid prototyping, injection moulds, milling and laser-cutting can be adapted for paperclay, merging the aesthetic and practical concerns of applied design with art practice. Sawing and cutting paperclay with power tools was introduced on p. 68, but we will see more variations in chapters ahead. In recent years, artists have been researching affordable ways to quickly translate 3D computer-modelled designs into ceramic, plaster, or other forms of media. Shapeways (www.shapeways.com) offers a service whereby digital-savvy artists can initiate a 3D form in a computer program and then hire them to build it in a range of media, including ceramic.

The designers and engineers of the future who adapt the non-linear design approach can use new assembly and forming methods with paperclay, which will

Make your own stamp. I carved my stamps and let them dry; dry paperclay is strong enough without firing. Here are some of my dry stamps, shown with the soft paperclay impression. *Photo: Gayle St Luise.*

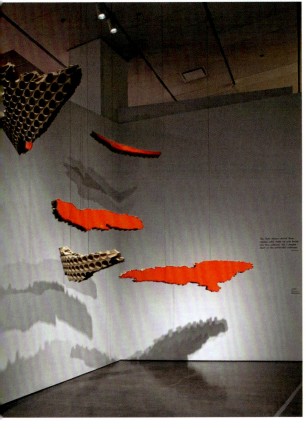

ABOVE: Neil Forrest and Team (USA), *Flake* installation, 2011. Paperclay/synthetic fibre laminates and mixed media, CAD/CAM modelled sections, 20 x 30 x 10 cm (8 x 12 x 4 in.). *Photo: Denver, Colorado Art Museum.*

RIGHT: Brian Gillis and Mike Miller, Ivy Study EIGER lab (USA), 2010. Three-dimensional printed paperclay casts from selective laser sintered paperclay moulds. *Photo: Mike Miller.*

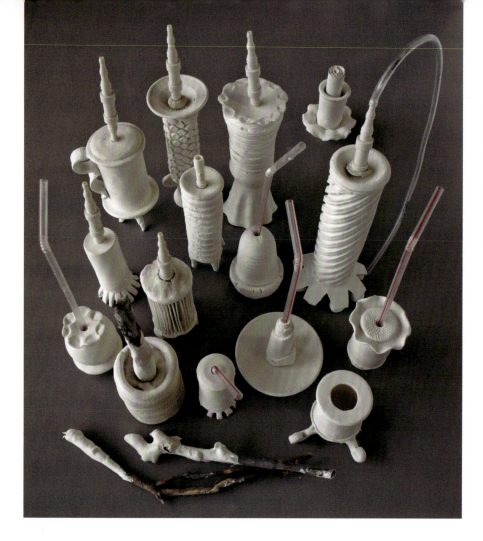

Water filter models by the author: wheel-thrown, hand-built, dipped. Low-cost, low-tech, earth-friendly solutions for clean drinking water are still critically needed in the developing world. Research is underway to use ceramic paperclay in water filter design. *Photo: Rosette Gault.*

lead to cost savings and the streamlining of manufacturing methods, just as artists have done.

My early research suggests that there are many new ways to make products that will evolve from the ideas presented in this book. For example, a fresh-cast or machined wet paperclay lid can be sized so that it will shrink and clamp in place over a dry paperclay container. The dimensions of the cast lid can be sized to allow this and the dry paperclay is strong enough to withstand the force. Rapid prototyping methods can be adapted too. More research is needed to further develop the field of sustainable materials involving recycled or reclaimed materials.

To illustrate some developing possibilities, the dry-to-dry assembly process for a large CAD-integrated ceramic structure *Heart Beats in Madrid 2011* used a sequential system of assembly for a complex, dry-parts-supported ceramic sculpture. The project was designed by Saeta Estudi of Barcelona for a special installation at ROCA Madrid Gallery in Spring 2011. You can view a two-minute video to get a sense of the making process at www.youtube.com/watch?v=6Bxbs2NAjgY.

Half a dozen life-size sculptures of porcelain non-grog paperclay were built in a week and a half. Front and back shells were press-moulded in the same sand-cast plaster mould so the source shape (theme) would be similar. To make the variations, leathersoft slabs were draped over the contour of the dry standing figures, but I let the new parts dry in place before attaching them. Other slab attachments for the arms and legs were dried separately on the floor or plaster slab, then joined using wet-to-dry methods. *Photo: Rosette Gault.*

Example of integrating methods: The Muses of Aliso Creek

Using a non-linear making approach will save months in a big project. I had half a dozen life-size sculptures built, dry and ready to fire in a week and a half using just a single set of sand-cast plaster slump press moulds. If I had more moulds, it would have been even faster.

Each night I force-dried the leathersoft porcelain slabs pressed into the set of open-face plaster moulds. I used a box fan aimed from the base up the centre. If the shells were not quite dry by morning, I turned them over with the top edge flush to the floor to keep the leatherhard paperclay from warping in the last stages of drying in the open air. I then repeated the press mould process right away, and was able to quickly produce and finish enough sets to assemble. We saw in Chapter 5 how dry porcelain shells like these are easy to store, transport and assemble (see p. 68) and how dry shells can be tacked in place with soft paperclay point wads (see p. 63, top left). I force-dried the wet parts between each work period so that joins and parts returned to maximum possible tensile strength and dryness during the process.

Fresh leathersoft drapes were allowed to shrink-dry in place before attaching. I wiped down and trimmed the edges of the dry, stable shells with a damp sponge then used little balls of soft clay underneath, as bumpers to steady the alignment between the rigid dry drapes and the dry form. The fresh point wads dried quickly. I filled in the gaps in vulnerable areas with soft, high-pulp paperclay slip and used a stable surface to apply colour and/or contour. The interiors of all the forms were mostly dry already, so they were ready to fire within a day or two. Traditional clay assembly at this size would require slow drying for weeks or months before firing could occur. Also, with large forms like these, I use scraps of dry clay for shims and wedges at the base, with soft paperclay to maintain balance.

Soak the bisque areas in the vicinity of the join in water for a moment. Then coat them with layers of thin paperclay slip or the soft, wet paste of paperclay. Attach the new part and let it dry in the open air and then check for hairline cracks. If the join is weight-bearing, bisque fire again to check it, or patch before firing at higher temperatures. *Photo: Rosette Gault.*

Combinations involving raw and fired paperclay

It is possible to embed already fired and glazed ceramic pieces in thick and wet paperclay slip and fire this intact (though if you fire beyond the temperature of the glazed pieces, then the glaze will tend to run). Today paperclay and paperclay slip are used for combinations between raw and fired work as well as mixed media. Methods for dipping (pp. 34–8) can be adapted for fired parts. Low-bisque and sinter-fired paperclay can be carved, and joined or embedded with raw paperclay, and these too will fire intact (p. 131).

Because of the ease of coating bisque surfaces with paperclay slip, repairing bisque cracks or adding unfired sections to bisque is possible, though not ideal. Repairs to dry cracks have a much higher success rate than those to bisque. Nevertheless, should you want to try it, first soak the areas needing repair in water for a moment. Then coat them with layers of thin paperclay slip and/or the soft, wet paste of paperclay. Bisque ware will accept multiple coatings of either.

Some types of hairline drying or firing cracks are not worth the trouble or require skill, patience and a little practice to repair. It depends where they are and why they have appeared. The typical cause is a low volume of pulp followed by stress or overwork at the leathersoft stage. You will need to make a judgement call on these cracks. Generally, it is worth trying to repair them, since the work will have to be started over if you do not (see also p. 32).

Julia Nema (Hungary), *Lumiverse 1,* 2010. Wood-fired translucent porcelain paperclay, 18 x 61 x 13 cm (7 x 24 x 5 in.). Exhibited at Armstrongs Gallery, USA. *Photo: Cynthia Madrigal.*

RIGHT: Susan Shultz works
are press moulded and then
hand modelled, altered and
detailed to a custom form.
Photo: Dean Powell.

BELOW: Tine Deweerdt
(Begium), *Structures
in Porcelain*, 2011.
Porcelain paperclay,
25 x 43 cm (10 x 17 in.).
Photo: Jean Godecharle.

7

Figures: small and large

The full repertoire of skills from both traditional sculpture practice and the ceramic legacy are merged when modelling figures in paperclay. Those who have learned to model in wax, oil-based clay, soft plaster and paste porcelain will notice similarities, as will those who know how to carve figures out of wood or stone. Traditional clay modelling methods, in which all parts are assembled when wet and leatherhard, could be used for a figure in paperclay, but this is not the only choice available. The chance to integrate dry and wet modelling offers opportunities to continue making changes and refinements through almost the whole making process.

Small scale: the maquette or miniature

Small-scale maquettes and figurines are far easier to transport, fire, display and store than large-scale works. When glazed and fired they can stand alone as a finished work or complement a larger work. It is also practical for studio artists to work out large-scale ideas and visions with maquettes first. Some maquettes may never be finished, fired works.

LEFT: Amanda Shelsher (Australia), *Not Drowning, Waving*, 2011. Earthenware paperclay, 35 x 55 x 25 cm (14 x 22 x 10 in.). *Photo: Bill Shaylor.*

RIGHT: Sue Stewart (Australia), *Friends*, 2003. Earthenware paperclay, 30 x 23 x 10 cm (11¾ x 9 x 4 in.). *Photo: Sue Stewart.*

Mark Nathan Stafford (USA), *Steeped*, 2010. The head is also a teapot. Cold steam, produced by an ultrasonic nebuliser and exhausted by a small fan, escapes from the ears and eyes. Paperclay installation, 137 x 54 x 76 cm (54 x 30 x 54 in.). *Photo: Mark Nathan Stafford.*

A paperclay maquette, when dry, is almost as tough as plaster. You can make changes to your dry maquette without having to start the whole work over or disturb the parts that don't need to change. You can draw marks and grid lines on the dry model if needs be. The model can also be slaked down when you're finished with it, or glazed and fired if you wish to keep it.

Familiar pinch, coil and slab-building techniques are commonly used to get the maquette started and form the elements of the figure. A base or pedestal can be made separately and joined to the figure when dry. A paperclay pedestal could start as a cut-out shape from a leathersoft slab, or even a coiled or pinched bowl turned upside-down.

Using the non-linear approach, dry strength helps support the form and delicate parts can be added, subtracted or changed even after they're dry. A soft, little figure may be too floppy to stand at first. It will dry out and harden within a day or so indoors, or perhaps an hour if placed in direct sun. Lay out leatherhard figures flat or in a pose, maybe propping the still-soft arms or legs. Lean them on something hard, such as a dry piece of paperclay, or drape them in a good position and let them dry out completely, at which point they will be strong enough to stand upright. If a figure needs shoes or feet, attach them to the dry form with a soft wad of paperclay or paperclay slip. To see how it will stand, you can tack it to the new, dry pedestal with soft clay. You can take it on and off the pedestal to work it many times. Once dry, areas can be re-softened with water to make refinements, without disturbing other dry parts. Model soft, wet paperclay features over the dry areas with tools such as a fettling blade, needle or sharp stick.

ABOVE LEFT: J. Alex Potter (USA), *Pluto*, 2010. Paperclay, 51 x 51 x 33 cm (20 x 20 x 13 in.). 'Paperclay allows unlimited expressive detail.' *Photo: J. Alex Potter.*

ABOVE RIGHT: Constance McBride (USA), *Will There Ever Be Peace* (detail), 2011. Paperclay, 53 x 112 x 43 cm (21 x 44 x 17 in.). *Photo: Michael Healy.*

RIGHT: Scarlett Kanistanaux (USA), *Such a Journey*, 2011. Stoneware paperclay. *Photo: courtesy of Scarlett Kanistanaux.*

Jiri Lonski (Czech Republic), *The Inner Life: Cries and Whispers*, 2003. Glazed earthenware paperclay with mixed-media cages inside, left: 81 x 53 x 28 cm (32 x 21 x 11 in.), right: 84 x 48 x 28 cm (33 x 19 x 11 in.). *Photo: Jiri Lonsky.*

Anjani Khanna (India), *Yali*, 2004. Stoneware paperclay with oxides, height: approx. 1.5 m (5 ft.). *Photo: Anjani Khanna.*

Should a figure need 'clothes', you may cut flat patterns, like those used for doll's clothes, in a leathersoft slab and drape, wrap or fold these over the dry figure. As explained previously (p. 52), I normally wait to attach them until these drapes are as dry as the figure beneath them for a more precise fit. Let parts and joins dry between sessions, then carve down or build up as needed. If a piece breaks, such as an ear or a finger, it's easy to make a new one, attach it and blend it in. Small figures can stand as they are or be transformed into structural armatures that feature moveable joints. These 'puppet armatures' are explained in Chapter 8 (pp. 95–6).

Large-scale projects

Advance planning for a large project will save a great deal of trouble before and after firing. Though not all projects need it, a maquette or scale model of the intended work can be most helpful. A set of small-scale variations can be prepared first before settling on the best version. In addition, a design plan allows me to coordinate tasks and give forethought to practicalities: for example, planning the size of templates, components, castings and sections in advance to fit into available kilns, through doors and inside vehicles and shipping crates. This document gives you a chance to think practical details through. If the work is going to be placed outdoors, how will its surfaces best be cleaned? This could be a factor in your selection of patina and glaze. How will it be installed or mounted? Is there a plan for de-install and relocation? Required openings, handles and reinforcement for transport or installation can be built into the structure. A list of items for consideration in a design document is supplied for your reference on p. 155.

Notes on scaling up

Many artists select the best of a series of maquettes to scale up for a larger version. The big version might be made not just of paperclay, but with bronze, cement or other weather-tolerant media. In paperclay, we adapt the traditional systems for scaling up sculpture. A dry paperclay maquette is strong enough to be marked up with gridlines, and these transposed onto the larger-scale replica. Or it is possible to work out the proportions with small-scale paper cut-out templates, which can be photocopied for scaling up. An image, silhouette or grid might be projected onto sheets of paper (or even paperclay) tacked up on a wall or laid out on the floor. Template guides are a real time-saver for a team of helpers when multiple sculptures are wanted. If a section breaks or you change your mind, a perfectly fitting replacement is quick to make.

Full details of the process for scaling up can be found in traditional sculpture how-to books. Most strategies can be applied for paperclay, too.

The modelling process

We know that parts can be made, detailed and dried separately before assembly. Detail on the face, for example, can be attended to with the head section oriented in a position that is comfortable and convenient, such as the artist's lap or a table-top. Some makers place a torso part or figure-in-progress on a Lazy Susan (a large rotating serving tray), banding wheel or a platform with casters. This way, it is possible to turn the work and inspect all sides of the figure without having to walk around it.

BELOW LEFT: Scott Douglas (USA) models fresh wet and soft-paste paperclay over a dry life-size casting made from porcelain paperclay. The casting is from a plaster mould of his face. *Photo: Rosette Gault.*

BELOW RIGHT: Ann Marais (South Africa), *Sorted*, 2009. Paperclay sculpture, height: 86 cm (34 in.). *Photo: Ann Marais.*

You can soften up spot areas for modelling by re-wetting them, as we discussed in Chapter 5 (pp. 57–8). I model over dry or leatherhard paperclay with very soft paste-like paperclay. Later, when the paste turns hard and dry, I can use carving techniques to achive both soft and hard details – sharp, crisp chiselling, or softer skin. I alternate addition and subtraction in stages until the contour fits the piece. The level of increasing detail is done in layers, as if I am focusing the lens of a camera.

Michelle Collier (USA) explains the spirit of her working process: 'If the piece needs major revision I sometimes use a rubber mallet to knock it apart so that I can recombine the pieces using slip and wet clay. I have even added elements to a previously-fired piece. Paperclay allows me to break the rules of traditional clay sculpting.'

Support

Artists have found new ways to put the strength of paperclay to use for internal support and the next chapter is devoted to the use of paperclay armatures inside paperclay sculpture. A stable axis is often needed to support the weight of a 'head', while allowing the head and neck to rotate, so a paperclay tube, or set of nesting tubes like those shown in the photo on p. 94, are strong enough to keep the head and neck connected loosely while still holding them upright from within. The neck and head can be temporarily tacked to the top of one of the tubes on a rim of soft paperclay or point wads, so you can loosely rotate the head and look at it from many possible angles.

Where a tube is hidden inside to lend stability and support to the heavier parts above, it should be long enough to connect with the base or ground level. This support tube should be thick-walled enough to support the weight of new parts above. Also, this inner column (like a backbone) should be thick enough that it will not get waterlogged from too much wet work. If you see a supporting tube softening too

ABOVE LEFT: Layers of very soft paperclay can be pressed, paddled and modelled over the top of a hollow torso, made from dry, folded slab cut-outs. *Photo: Rosette Gault.*

ABOVE RIGHT: Here, soft paperclay pressed in a single, dry paperclay mould (far right) has resulted in a family of clone-like dry castings. In the soft paperclay I model and fettle changes in facial expression, hair, sex, eyes, lips, nose and bone structure for each, wet over dry. This method can be scaled up for life-size masks. Porcelain paperclay, work in progress, by the author. *Photo: Gayle St Luise.*

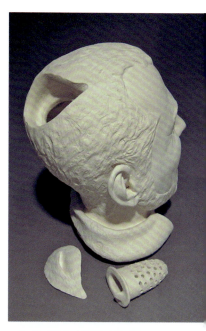

Mark Nathan Stafford (USA), teapot special effects, work in progress, 2009. Porcelain paperclay, 28 x 18 x 23 cm (11 x 7 x 9 in.). Engineer a close fit between dry, interior parts, leaving enough space to fit a small fan and nebuliser for special effects. The steam from the teapot water is designed to come out through the eyes and ears on demand. The interior is kept open so parts can dry completely between sessions. It will be closed in for detailing the join and surfaces before firing. In the top right, we see another head/teapot in progress, with a nesting tea strainer and cap shown in the foreground. *Photo: Mark Nathan Stafford.*

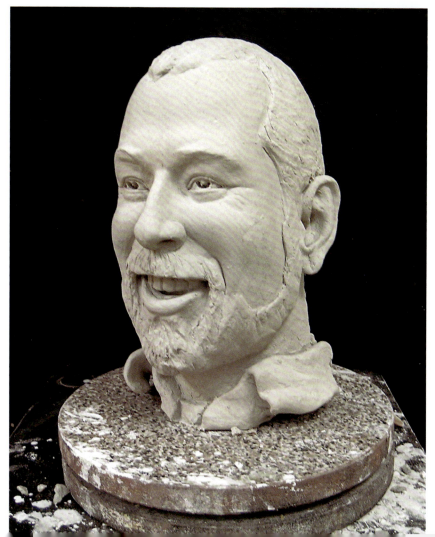

Plan the best way for various parts to fit together and check this before firing. Build a custom axis so that the head can be rotated to the angle desired. Think ahead; if parts will be fired separately and reassembled, ensure to fit loosely enough that there is space for temporary or permanent putty or adhesive for installing or de-installing. Work in progress, Mark Nathan Stafford (USA). *Photo: Mark Nathan Stafford.*

ABOVE: This work started with a central column of dry paperclay tubes, threaded over a wooden pole to stabilise them while the new elements were added. With wet to dry assembly methods, it is possible to create and then match 'keys' or 'tabs' to easily hook between each section. Later, the stacking elements were lifted off the pole, fired and transported separately, and assembled again on site. Work in progress, Pirjo Pesonen (Finland). *Photo: Rosette Gault.*

much, the remedy is easy: stop, and let your structure dry hard again overnight or over a few hours, removing the head if necessary to speed drying. This interval will give you enough time to attend to another element or thicken up the weak part.

An alternative to a paperclay tube is to slide a wooden dowel stick down the neck. You will need to remove it before the neck is finally attached, toward the end of your project.

You can invent or customise props or shims at the base of the sculpture with some dry wedges of paperclay too. As figures scale up to life-size forms that will be fired in a kiln, reinforcement and back-up props can be added at any time in the process. We will discuss strategies for reinforcement and structure in the next chapter.

Finishing up

A completed life-size paperclay figure is usually dry enough to fire within a day or two. Wet joins between dry parts dry quickly and the interior structure will have been dried periodically throughout most of the construction.

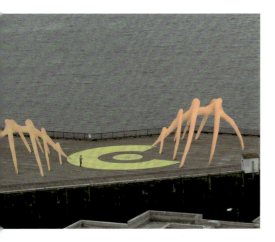

ABOVE: Proposal models by Rosette Gault for sculptures at the helicopter target, Seattle Waterfront Park Pier 52/53, 2012. Smaller versions were prepared and images of the models superimposed over my photo of the site so I could calculate how much to scale up, how much clay would be needed, logistics and costs in advance. This proposal was on display at Seattle Tacoma International Airport in 2012. *Photo: Rosette Gault.*

ABOVE: Michelle Collier (USA), *Where do we come from*, 2010. Paperclay ceramic, 61 x 28 x 23 cm (24 x 11 x 9 in.). *Photo: Dana Davis.*

LEFT: Avery Palmer (USA), *The Man in the Moon*, 2008. Earthenware and paperclay, 40.5 x 35.5 x 15 cm (16 x 14 x 6 in.). *Photo: Avery Palmer.*

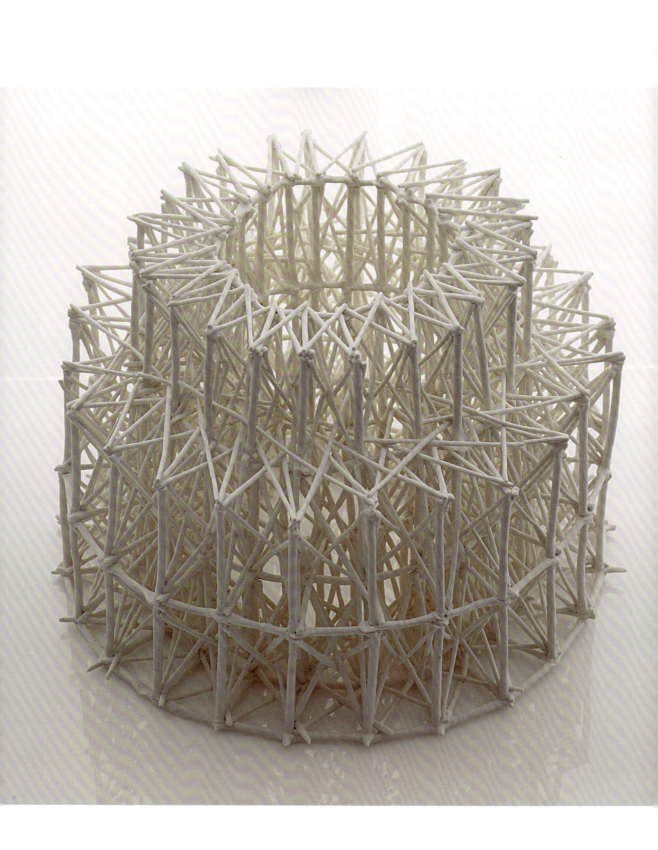

Structure and armatures

In this chapter we will look at choices for support and structural reinforcement for paperclay. An armature structure for paperclay can be planned or improvised. No matter whether you work in a 'tidy' or a 'messy' way, you have choices about how to assemble the simplest or most complex of armatures. Like many paperclay artists, I take inspiration for armature structures from nature: the bones of vertebrates and invertebrates, honeycombs, nests, webs and the like. I use a mixture of principles from architecture, engineering and my own common sense.

Practices adapted from traditional methods

'Hump and slump' systems from traditional ceramics can provide effective support for leathersoft paperclay until it stiffens. The idea is to drape paperclay slabs, ribbons, tubes or folds over (hump) or inside (slump) a rigid form. We saw variations on this in Chapter 4. The shape is removed once the paperclay hardens to a shell. A variation from the traditional method is to fill a sock or bag with shredded or crumpled paper, spongy foam, grains, sand or other material. If you wrap or drape soft paperclay over and around this, leave a hand-sized exit hole. After the paperclay dries, this will allow room to empty the stuffing out and gently remove the sock or bag. This leaves a hollow shell of dry paperclay. Thérèrse LeBrun further developed this method for her own special paperclay practice (p. 35, top left).

LEFT: Nuala O'Donavan, (Ireland), *Radiolaria*, 2012. Porcelain paperclay 43 x 42 x 28 cm (17 x 16½ x 11 in.). *Photo: Sylvain Deleu.*

RIGHT: Madhvi Subrahmanian in her studio, Fost Gallery, Singapore. A complex lattice can be built up in stages, with time to dry between work periods. *Photo: Stephanie Fong.*

LEFT: Del Harrow (USA), *Bone Scaffolding*, 2011. Slip-cast porcelain (with mixed fibre addition), glaze, platinum lustre, 36 x 48 x 89 cm (14 x 19 x 35 in.). 'This CAD designed form is a modular system made up of slip-cast components, fired separately, that can be assembled into either a free-standing sculpture or a porous wall or architectural screen.' *Photo: Del Harrow.*

BELOW: Improvise the structure of a support frame. After new parts are added to the frame and are dry, re-check the balance and integrity of the joins. Work in progress, Malene Pedersen (Denmark). *Photo: Malene Pedersen.*

What is an armature?

In sculpture, an armature is a frame or surface used to support soft, pliant modelling material like wax or plasticine, as well as oil-based clay, plaster, fibreglass or rubber. As no kiln is involved in mixed media sculpture, the armature could be a material such as wood, metal, wire, mesh or foam, hidden inside the form. There are even re-useable wood or metal figure armatures available for purchase, with elaborate flexing ball-and-socket metal joints. In fashion, tailors use adjustable 'dress forms' for solid support when fitting dresses and suits.

Soft paperclay can mimic many of these non-clay materials and dry paperclay proves strong enough to function as an armature by itself. We will see some instances of how artists use it in this chapter.

When do you need an armature?

On a small scale or with a simple vessel form, an armature may not be needed. But as paperclay ceramic works scale up and get heavier, or walls get paper-thin, provisions for internal support may be needed and can be built in as you go. The larger and more

Armatures inspired by nature. Designs based on plant forms are seen in cross-section to illustrate how one central tube could slide inside the other, with minimal increase in weight. Tubes could be custom-fitted inside a sculpture after the outside shell is dry, but wait to seal until they are as dry as the outside shell to attach them into final position.
Photo: Rosette Gault.

complex the work, the more functional a built-in framework can be before and after firing. Not only can the internal 'bones' of this structure be fitted with precision to match the form, but the paperclay frame can be permanent or temporary, internal or external, exposed or covered completely.

As the scale increases, the chance of over-firing some parts also increases. Traditionally, works were put in saggar pots to limit the slumping and warping that might occur. A bulky brick can be fired next to the work as a safety prop (see p. 128). But as an alternative to using kiln posts or bricks as a prop, a paperclay structure resembling scaffolding can be built, which will stand around the work to prop it through the firing and can be removed afterward.

Types of paperclay armature

There are several workable strategies for starting and building an armature:

A. Build a frame from the inside out. We will look at the principles behind the 'tube frame' method used for larger projects and the string armature (the 'puppet' method), which features moveable joints, and might be used for smaller forms.

B. Build a dry shell exterior first, then fit a frame inside it.

C. Improvise a structure that mixes A and B. (You can only really improvise once you understand and have tested the two previous methods.)

Method A: Build a frame from the inside out

This method involves creating a stable central column or frame that can support additions of soft paperclay over it. The interior frame is initially assembled by joining dry paperclay parts, such as hollow tubes or hemispheres, tapered cones, rolls or folded slabs. Once

An assortment of dry, folded parts, seen to the left, will be assembled and reinforced with thick high-pulp paperclay slip and soft paperclay in between them. In the foreground, I am filling the area around the tube in the base underneath the vest form. Though I could just as easily cover all of the base neatly, here I might leave the central support tube open to more easily mount the bust on a base after firing. At the top of this tube will be the neck. A clear bowl of water shows where the heavy head will sit, with soft wads of clay between until the best angle is decided and final joins are made. Even loosely-made nesting tubes are better filled in when dry than when they are soft. *Photo: Gayle St Luise.*

a structure exists, it can then be built over. Though a solid coil of high-pulp paperclay could be used (around 5–10 cm, or 2–4. in. in diameter), hollow tubes are far stronger for building armatures. For an example of how strong a tube structure can be, look at the large wind-powered 'Strandebeest' structures of Theo Jansen, moving along the beach in Holland (you can see them here: www.youtube.com/watch?v=HSKyHmjyrkA). These 'armatures in motion' are built almost completely from lightweight PVC plumbing pipes. A life-size paperclay form can expand and contract gently through the stress of drying, wetting and firing, and hollow tubes will lighten the weight.

Folded slab cut-outs can be an even faster way to create volume and yet still support weight from a torso or head above. The various parts needed to support a torso can be made separately and fitted together when dry; see the dry parts laid out in the picture above. Thicker curves should be strong enough to support many layers of soft paperclay over the top, and as much drilling, chiselling and carving down as your project might need. It is wise to wait for joins to dry and become very strong before beginning to add heavy layers above them.

For a more advanced structure, the assembly process is likely to proceed in steps. For the abstract skeleton form shown on p. 51, I connected a set of five dry and tapered hollow arches with soft paperclay and paperclay slip at the intersections. At first, each new, wet joint could 'flex', so I was free to adjust these to find the best place for them. After the new joins set and dried completely, the frame was stable even on dry, pointy feet.

Next, I dropped a thin 'skin' of soft paperclay from several feet above. When it landed on the dry frame, it stretched enough to capture some contour from the backbone and ribs underneath. This soft slab was left undisturbed to dry and shrink in place before I connected it to the frame. As the dry paperclay is at its maximum strength, this is the best time at which to reinforce the joins, add contours or add soft wet extensions.

Some armature assemblies turn out to be dynamic sculptures all on their own. The work of Nuala O'Donovan (see pp. 90 and 92) gives example of structures of many parts, each measured, assembled and balanced with imagination and skill.

An example of an improvised support structure. Many hollow tubes have been added to support at the back of thin paperclay slabs in the neck and arms, visible here. The new joins have dried in place. I added curved slabs to widen the hips. When all is dry again, I fill or cover over these and any visible seams with thicker high-pulp soft paperclay. Air pockets inside are OK in paperclay construction. Multiple episodes of re-wetting and drying (overnight or in the sun) are key to assembling the piece in days rather than months. Research works in progress (life-size) by the author, Limoges porcelain non-grog paperclay. With support from the International Ceramics Research Center, Guldagergaard, Denmark, 2009. *Photo: Rosette Gault.*

Puppet system: string armatures

A string armature is another system of building from the inside out that I have researched and adapted for paperclay figure work. It gives moveable joints on figures and makes it easier to repair delicate broken parts. It can also be an alternative to building a framework of tubes or slabs. String is best to use for this, rather than wire, because the string burns out in firing and leaves an interior 'hollow', beneficial for air circulation, tensile strength and more (pp. 34–5).

When natural-fibre string is coated in paperclay slip to build up thick layers, like a candle, the result will dry hard enough to stand upright. Wet, coated string will not stand by itself and will also stick to dry paperclay, itself, cloth and bisque, so must be arranged in a flat shape on a tabletop or hung or draped somewhere until it dries. Some artists drape their dipped string over balloons and plastic to get curved lines.

For a quick and mobile puppet, cut and knot a stick figure out of some string, twine or rope. Dip this in slip multiple times to build up layers. Wait for the paperclay slip to set or even to dry completely between dips. Prop or hang the wet string in the desired position until it dries, so that the arms, legs and head are not tangled and are in a gesture you like.

To get the effect of a flexing joint on a dry string figure, score a guideline at the desired location for the joint with a needle and bend it gently open. The string

will be peeking through and pliant, unlike the stiff, dry paperclay. Don't tear, yank or cut through the string. If cutting joints in the string figure causes the figure to become floppy, tack a wad of very soft paperclay into the joints to hold them. When these dry, the desired gesture will be fixed. Press soft clay on top of and around the string to fatten contours if you like. The coating of paperclay slip on the dipped string should be thicker than 2–3 mm. The fired result will be extremely fragile if the coating is too thin.

Method B: Dry shell exterior first, then a frame inside it

To build this way, reverse the sequence described for Method A. Create the exterior shell or skin first, then fit ribs and cross braces inside. The project could start with a simple dry shell of paperclay on its side or upright, a draped or folded slab, a coiled form, a cast form, or any combination one can imagine.

There are many possible designs for custom-built cross-bracing. For internal cross-bracing, paperclay tubes or 'half-rounds' (a tube sliced or folded lengthwise) are usually stronger than a single coil or strips. Drape soft, fresh tubes or half-rounds inside the dry shell or vessel. Arrange, fit and trim the tubes – which look like ribs, a spine or a lattice – so they will dry in the shape of the shell's curves. Then attach them to the shell when they are dry. Frames with structural symmetry are not the only possibility; example of works in progress are shown opposite, and on p. 99. The larger the scale, the more I integrate structural engineering principles into my construction process.

After the new parts dry completely, it is fast and easy to attach them either to each other or to the shell as you please. Brush a generous amount of paperclay slip in and around the point of contact. Alternatively, the dry bracing can be quickly dipped in a

ABOVE LEFT: Dane Youngren (USA), works in progress. Handbuilt stoneware paperclay structures inspired by abandoned mining shafts in western North America. *Photo: Rosette Gault.*

ABOVE RIGHT: Even though the details are unfinished, dry dipped string figures can be placed in a scene and gestures explored. Layers of soft paperclay pressed over and around the dry string make legs and feet strong. Dabs of paperclay slip join and anchor figures securely. The central, seated figure is a string armature that had flexible joints, which have now been filled in. It has been contoured and detailed more than the others. Work in progress by author. *Photo: Gayle St Luise.*

RIGHT: Arranging leathersoft tubes in a dry paperclay shell. Let the 'ribs' dry and shrink slightly down into position to fit the contour exactly. When both tubes and the shell are dry and stable, begin to join them with wet, soft paste, clay or slip in any combination. My research indicates that symmetrical internal structures are most stable. Limoges porcelain paperclay, work in progress by the author. *Photo: Rosette Gault.*

LEFT AND RIGHT: Here you can see reinforcement and cross-bracing in the waist section, using a tube structure. Much later, after I closed both sides of the figure, I decided to change it again. I removed sections of the shell covering to expose some of the interior 'bones' and was free to add and subtract until satisfied. Limoges porcelain paperclay, ungrogged, work in progress. Research by author, carried out at the International Ceramic Center, Guldagergaard, Denmark. *Photo: Rosette Gault.*

Labels in image:
1 — Point wads
2 — 3 layers, wet-dry
8 — Low pulp
3 — Thick slip inside
4
7 — High pulp
5 — Single thick coat
6 — Applying second coat
High-fired porcelain

The thicker you go, the more pulp you may need

I made a set of dry rings to mimic a cross-section view of a support tube that might be used to build armatures and to observe the wet-to-dry bond with layers of paperclay slip. I applied layers of thick paperclay slip to the inside or outside of each ring. To observe the amount of natural torque and adhesion in drying I did not pre-score the smooth surface on the ring for the test. In the image, I am adding a second thick coat over dry to 6. A single thick coat has been added to 5, and in 7, two thick coats have dried tightly around the ring, with no cracks appearing between seams. The thick, low-pulp slip (8) cracked a little, as expected, but can still be patched. 1 and 2 show how some soft paperclay point wads hold two dry rings. Thick paperclay applied to the inside of a dry ring pulled away a little in 3, but did not do this in 4, likely because I spent a bit more time pressing it in place. Research by author.
Photo: Gayle St Luise.

bucket of paperclay slip and placed in the dry shell; it will grip quite well. Fill in and around the gaps with soft paperclay or paperclay slip and let this dry again. Sometimes I keep a supply of dry tubes on hand to cut and use as extra structural bracing. Dipping strips of paperclay in slip and wrapping them like bandages around the joints and lattice intersections is another way to reinforce the weight-bearing joins.

It is possible to fill the interior of a dry, thin shell exterior with several inches of thick, high-pulp paperclay slip or putty and keep internal structures to a minimum (see p. 94). The photo above illustrates in cross-section just how many extra inches of paperclay slip can be successfully added to a dry shell or tube to dry in place without cracks. Knowing this, filling dry paperclay shells can be part of a strategy for reinforcing a complex folded slab, like the the one we saw on p. 69.

BELOW: Allen Chen (USA), works in progress, 2009. Dip woven yarn into paperclay slip, dry, and then repeat until the structure is thick enough to support itself once paper has burned out. After the bisque firing (right), temporary support was removed. More layers of glaze were added and the piece was fired to higher temperatures before it was finished. *Photos: Allen Chen.*

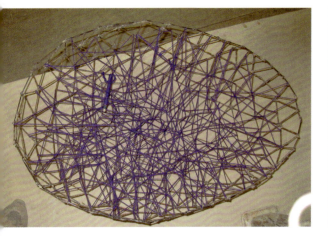

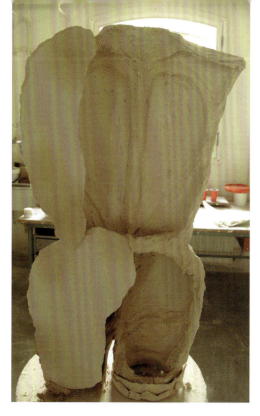

LEFT: Fast drying stabilises big porcelain paperclay works. Since paperclay is at its maximum tensile strength in the dry state, I dry my piece between work periods. You might see some dampness appear for a short time while secondary joints between the frame and the previously dry hooks are drying, but this evaporates quickly. Limoges porcelain paperclay, by the author. *Photo: Rosette Gault.*

ABOVE: I added wet handles, hooks, rings and ledges on the back of a dry section of flat slab and dried them in the sun. The handle must become as dry as the slab in order for it carry weight. I could hang the hook on the internal frame of a figure to preview how it was going to look or test its strength, or remove it like a door to get inside the new form. These flat pieces are shown hanging on the form on the left. *Photo: Rosette Gault.*

Large-scale frame assemblies

As work scales up in size, methods from architecture, building and structural engineering can be adapted for paperclay. Structures that combine the methods A and B are used by advanced practitioners (p. 93).

In the piece shown above, to close in the frame and cover the close fit of thin, slab arms, legs and chest securely for firing, I needed to make the covering panels hang but they had to be adjustable to fit the frame. I built custom hook handles, edges and ledges with a soft coil on the back side of each, but waited for the new weight-bearing joins to dry securely.

Multiple drying periods are key to setting weight-bearing joins. When dry, I tested the new clay ledges and hooks. To test them, I hung the dry 'arms' in position on the dry frame, pressing a few soft point wads underneath to tack them on. Later, I could unhook these big covering parts and make changes to them or to the frame. In this way it is possible for a big shape to be easily pried open if you need to get inside for last minute trimming or reinforcement, but just as easy to close it up when you're done. For example, it is often easier to apply colour and glaze to the interior of a big dry form while it is opened up.

Strategies for reinforcement at large-scale

Evaluate your dry structure for potential weaknesses at the start of each work period. Strengthen cracks when dry to reinforce them (p. 43). Add more support or thicken around and over weight-bearing joins, including the bottom rim, at the base.

Using shims at the base will help level a large work; add/subtract parts and the centre of gravity shifts. Shims, which can be made of chips or wedges of dry paperclay, are left loose. They can be easily sealed and merged with the base towards the end of the building process. Paying attention to balance and stability at the base can keep a thin-walled or very large work from tipping over or slumping during a high temperature firing.

In the photo on p. 69, dry folded Limoges porcelain slabs were arranged and tacked in place with spot joins using soft clay. It was fast and easy to change or move these to settle on a good arrangement.

Unless appropriate reinforcement is made, the thin neck of an assembly is at risk of warping during firing. Most large kilns will have hot spots and it is possible to accidentally over-fire. I look for room inside the neck and body, secure a custom-fit dry tube from top to bottom, and apply thick layers of slip to cover it. In the picture on p. 69, this vertical is just along the left side. After it dries I cover all my additions and joins with a fresh layer of high-pulp paperclay slip or paste so they will be lightweight after firing. I look at the open pockets around tacked-in joins, noting where and how many they are. These will become points of strength in the frame as they are filled and covered with paperclay slip or soft paperclay. The knees, feet and curled over sections are in obvious need of reinforcement as well.

Reinforcement of vulnerable forms

In the case of a torso or 'dry shell' made of thin, folded slabs intended to function as armature support, I can use some other strategies to thicken up or stabilise thin areas from behind. I might apply a criss-cross lattice of soft paperclay strips or coils, which have been dipped in papeclay slip (see opposite page). This also shows how tubes and folded slabs could be combined.

I can fit a dry temporary cross-bracing with internal props to keep large, upright slabs from buckling in the fire. When the work is dry and nearing completion, before it is fired, I also check that the base, rims and other areas that will experience post-firing wear and tear are just a bit thicker than normal.

Internal support for large-scale structures

When firing, areas where big, thin slabs arch over a span, such as under a neck that supports a heavy head, or where a clay slab stands upright on a thin edge and is at risk of warping inward at the middle, are potentially vulnerable.

If possible, anticipate any risk of deformation from a hot spot in the kiln. For example, to support an outstretched wing through the fire, consider building a scaffolding prop to fire with the piece, which can then be removed. You can read more on firing in Chapter 11. It might also make sense to design and fit an appendage, like a wing or an arm, so that it can be removed after firing for shipping and transport. All interlocking parts can be built, handled and tested at the dry stage.

Allen Chen (USA), *Rust Belt Transition: Installation*, 2010. Paperclay and glazes, fired. These works were started with a wire frame and yarn structure, coated many times with paperclay slip to build up contour, 33 x 33 x 25.5 cm (13 x 13 x 10 in.). *Photo: by the artist.*

Planning for outdoor work

If the piece is going to be kept outdoors, consider whether the internal or external structure needs drain paths so rain, ice or snow will have an exit hole and water will not be trapped in hidden pockets or gaps. There is a 99% chance that your paperclay will survive outdoor freezing and thawing if properly formulated and fired. An outdoor paperclay sculpture is shown in freezing conditions in the photos on pp. 140–1 in Chapter 12. But since base clays and firings vary so much, there can be no guarantees. It may help to deep-freeze/thaw a sample of your fired paperclay and glazes in advance a few times, to get a sense of what to expect from them.

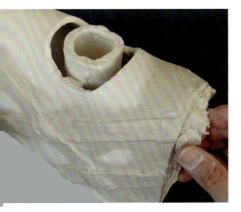

Sometimes a cross-lattice reinforcing frame can be improvised on the spot. Dip leathersoft paperclay strips in paperclay slip and apply them like tape, under or over a dry paperclay slab like this vest. The wetness on the dry slab will evaporate. Work in progress by the author. *Photo: Gayle St. Luise.*

Armature design and trimming notes

Paperclay armatures can be beautiful and tidy structures. Parts can be perfectly fitted in symmetrical, bilateral and graceful arrangements, and can have as much symmetry and dynamic balance as Alexander Calder's (1898–1976) hanging mobiles and scultures, balanced on fulcrums. Like the very best embroidery, the degree of craftsmanship applied to an armature could be so high that it's hard to tell front and back apart. Whatever method suits you, finish the dry structure neatly by smoothing over with thin paperclay slip and wiping down with a damp sponge.

Artists with a more improvisational style will hardly fuss over the joins, giving dry tubes a quick dip in paperclay slip and sticking them in position in the midst of a jumble of props and point wads. A quick, thick smear of putty in the gaps might be enough to tack parts in place. With all this inner working, the work in progress can look very messy for a time. Again, a final coat of paperclay slip and a wipe-down will tidy and cover the tracks.

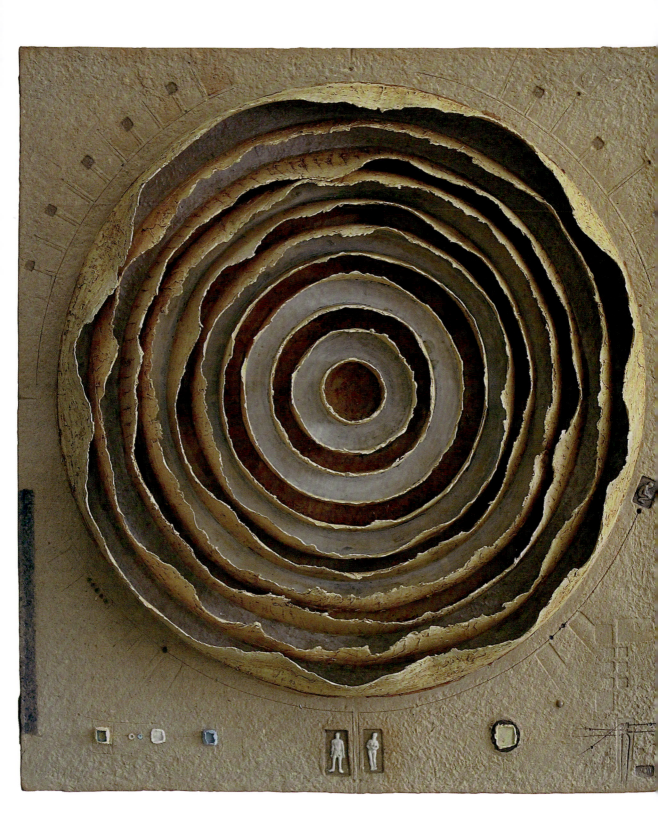

9 Tiles and panels

Paperclay is a good choice for tiles, wall hangings or murals because of its lighter fired weight. Single firing is feasible because the water-absorbent dry ware will accept glaze. Moreover, even thin, larger-sized panels can be trimmed and transported when they are dry. Though most artists want a thin panel, about 1–3 cm/½–1¼ in., 6–8 cm (2½–3¼ in.) or more can be achieved. The higher the pulp-to-clay ratio, the thicker and larger the tile can be. High-pulp paperclay wall panels can be fired flat. Thick texture and depth (about 5 cm/2 in.) can be next to thin (1 cm/½ in.) in the same work. We are now seeing thin, translucent, porcelain paperclay panels and tiles that can be glazed in a painterly way or in relief, and panels are being fired in wood or salt kilns.

Tiles or panels can be started by traditional methods with rolling pins and slab rollers (pp. 46–7), or by pouring paperclay slip over a plaster slab (pp. 41–3), into a frame, or pouring or pressing into a mould.

As we learned in Chapter 5, dry paperclay tiles or panels are strong enough to be moved and handled, to be carved into, and to build up contours and layers in. Their unfired strength allows big panels to be handled or stood on edge before firing. If anything happens to one of the tiles, they are quite easy to repair or replace. We have seen that if paperclay dries flat, it will usually stay flat, provided it is fired correctly and was handled correctly when initially made (see pp. 54–5). And as we discussed in the previous chapters, all the methods of cutting, joining, alteration and modelling of wet-

LEFT: Hasan Sahbaz (Turkey), *Places-Borders-Peoples* series, 2010. Stoneware paperclay, 49 x 46 x 7 cm (19¼ x 18 x 2¾ in.). *Photo: Erdal Tusun.*

RIGHT: Paul Chaleff (USA), installation of glazed panels in progress, 2010. Stoneware paperclay. *Photo: Paul Chaleff.*

on-dry can be integrated in the same piece. In addition to the ability to contour and model low reliefs with wet-on-dry methods, artists can transfer images and tracing guides to paperclay tiles. The surface can be painted, screenprinted or drawn on as if it is a canvas, whether it is dry or wet, or at both stages in several layers. Paperclay tile projects range from single highlight tiles and trivets (p. 109), suitable for beginners to paint on, to more complex professional projects.

Maarit Makela (Finland), *Light*, 2007. Translucent porcelain paperclay with screenprinted glazed images, 40 x 98 cm (15¾ x 38½ in.). *Photo: Rauno Traskelin.*

Planning a tile layout

For a layout of wall tiles in any larger project, I first make a design plan from start to finish. In this way I can anticipate and integrate all steps of the process and facilitate the creation of each tile to fit in available kilns as well as merge well in the tile outline pattern in the design. I work out practical ways to transport, fire and install ahead of time. For large wall tiles or panels, I might consider a system for installing or de-installing them that is not as permanent as grout, such as velcro strips on the back. To make the finished work easier to clean throughout its life I might plan for a gloss or semi-gloss glaze finish. Alternatively, the effect of dirt on a porous matt surface may contribute to the desired result. See the Appendix for an example of design plan considerations (p. 155). When a paperclay tile is at the dry stage, the back side can be custom-fit to accept mounting installation hardware, by modelling with a coil of fresh wet clay and joining it wet to dry (p. 67).

First I measure the dimensions of the mural or tile layout on a scaled-down grid. For example, five small squares on the grid might represent a metre. Alternatively, one tile could be represented by one square on the grid, so if my mural will be four metres wide, I would sketch a frame that is 20 squares wide to represent this measure scaled down. I make my initial sketches using this as a guide and later convert it to scale. I usually make a full-scale paper template and either lay this over a frame bed of soft clay, or lay it on the floor and assemble the new tiles over it as I make them. With paperclay, the tiles need not all be made at the same time.

Cynthia Dahlstrom (USA),
Jungle Boogie, 1998.
Bas-relief: the cut lines
complement the mural
design; borders are tidy and
seem part of the work. Test
the fit of the tiles together
when they are dry. In this
case, the artist made a
template on the floor. She
planned the border and
set the birds and flowers
in position, then filled
in the mosaic of smaller
tiles around them. The
dry paperclay was easy to
handle and did not warp.
Photo: Cynthia Dahlstrom.

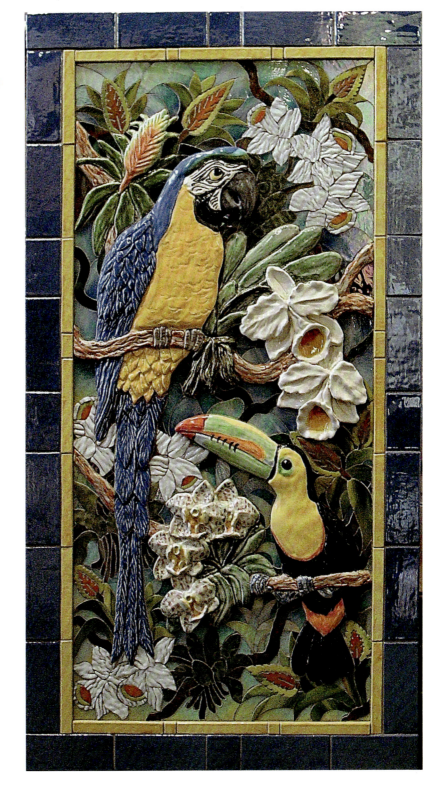

Because a layout of close-fitting dry tiles will shrink in firing from the original wet measure, it makes sense to design a template for cutting the wet tiles in a frame, scaled a bit larger than the finished measurements. Since the shrinkage of each base clay varies, if you want or need to know precisely how much shrinkage to expect, scribe a 10 cm line in a test tile of soft paperclay. After the tile dries, measure the change in the length of the line. Then fire the tile and again compare the lines. The wet to dry to fired shrinkage tends to range between 2 and 20%, and the shrinkage is easy to calculate if you use 10 cm to start with. In practice, this means a framed layout of paperclay tiles, planned for the size you intended, will shrink down and leave enough uniform space between each tile for grout and tile spacers if you are planning a permanent setting.

When feasible, make a full-sized frame and create a bed of leathersoft or poured paperclay as one unit first. The plan ideally will be to let all the tiles dry as a unit, even with cut-lines started, in the open air on an absorbent surface like plaster. This tends to keep the individual tiles' edges from curling during drying. However, before the leatherhard stage, consider making the cut lines for the tiles just part-way with a needle or sharp knife in the clay bed, and finish the cut when it is totally dry. Then you can snap or cut dry tiles apart with little risk of them warping (see p. 67). When the paperclay can be safely handled, trim and clean up the edges by wiping down with a damp sponge. To get a better sense of the fit, set dry tiles in the frame again, leaving a little space between each for grout.

In Chapter 5, we discussed how to make and finish crisp edges, repairs and detail. At this stage, the dry and absorbent surface can be prepared for further glazing and colour too. Or, using the non-linear method, fresh joins and layers can be added if needed.

Most mural methods and design strategies can be adapted for paperclay, but of course many of the books covering these are based on traditional clay methods, so limitations in assembly between the wet and leatherhard stages are assumed. The paperclay artist does not have to obey all these rules!

Using a frame and pouring slip

For a big panel or mural, a wood frame can be constructed to act as a border for pouring paperclay slip. This method allows you to mix up very high-pulp mixtures that will fire lightweight, and to skip some intermediate steps, such as handling and making soft slabs of paperclay that have to be merged together.

Using this method, the frame is placed over a level, water-absorbent surface, like plaster or cement, on the floor or a flat surface. Mix up thick, high-pulp slip, maybe five buckets-full, and press a soft coil of paperclay at the seam between the floor and the work surface. Then pour one or more thick puddles of the paperclay slip into the frame and spread it to the edges, to a depth of at least 2 cm (¾ in.). I find it helpful to mark the 2 cm (¾ in.) measure on the frame with masking tape so I don't overfill it.

Once poured, check the depth of the setting paperclay in a couple of places with a probe or toothpick, also marked with a measuring line. As it dries, the soft paperclay

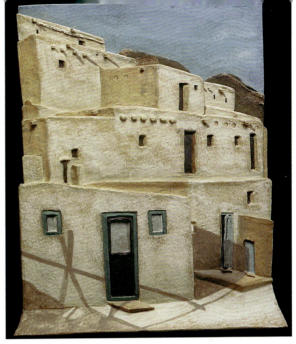

Cynthia Dahlstrom (USA), paperclay mural in progress, 1995. Here, curved cut-lines enhance the visual theme and straight cut-lines lead the viewer's eye to the centre, where the figure is. *Photo: Cynthia Dahlstrom.*

Jeanne Henry (USA), *Taos Pueblo, Light*, 2006. Paperclay, 38 x 51 x 5 cm (15 x 20 x 2 in.). *Photo: Jeanne Henry.*

can be cut into interlocking shapes. I might lay a grid or paper template over the new paperclay and mark some planned cut-lines for tiles at this time also.

To facilitate the 'release' of the new tiles from the surface when they are leatherhard or dry, an option may be to paint a thin coating of paperclay slip over the work surface and sides of the frame beforehand, but make sure this thin layer is completely dry before you start to pour over it.

Combinations of wet and dry for wall panels

Soft drapes can be blended into flat, dry panels using wet-on-dry processes. Skills for dry-wet and dry-dry joins were explained in Chapter 5. You can integrate any and all methods that might fit your working style, imagination and project.

An example of how thin, soft paperclay can be blended is shown in the photos at the top of p. 109. Here, a dry 'stalk' shape (a slab rolled into a tube) has been fixed to a dry panel. After that join dried completely, the stalk was detailed again with a new layer of fresh wet leaves and vines. The transition between two dimensions and three dimensions appears smooth and gradual and the illusion of foliage merged into the overall picture. In the central section, you have to look closely to detect that some thin edges from a leathersoft slab have been smoothed and blended into the dry, flat surface as part of the body of the frog. Furthermore, the artist applied just the right amount of colour by air-brushing over the relief.

Casting panels

For a series of large wall panels, Klaus Steindlmuller prepared a set of big plaster drying moulds, using surface texture from corrugated cardboard boxes, complete with folding wrinkles and creases (see opposite page). At slip and leathersoft stages, his paperclay wall panels took the impression of the cardboard texture from the plaster. He decorated the clay surface with colourful ceramic glaze.

Insertions and mosaics

Mosaic pieces of dry or glazed ceramic or paperclay can be inserted directly into a bed of high-pulp slip. We saw the beginning of the process in Chapter 3 (p. 30). Let the poured high-pulp slip dry around the pieces to fix them in place. Then pour or brush a new layer of high-pulp slip to fill in around gaps and level up the surface between the insertions. Wipe off the excess slip from the top of the mosaics with a damp sponge.

All forms of clay and paperclay can be placed in slip, pushed into soft paperclay or joined to dry paperclay. Some artists also place wire, metal, glass beads or marbles that give melted residues, puddles of cracked glass, flashing smoke trails and other special fired effects. The Belgian artist Thérèse LeBrun has adapted this multilayer mosaic method using seeds (p. 35). The seeds burn out to create extraordinary surface textures.

In some of my paperclay wall panels, I have embedded glazed and finished pot fragments and small figures directly in the wet paperclay slip of a large, thin wall panel. Colour is applied when the work is dry.

Household feature tiles

Not all artists will be making big panels, but the principles are the same for smaller tiles, such as hand-built 'feature' tiles for the home. These could be set among factory tiles or used on their own.

If you're not using a pouring method, tiles can be started by slicing a thick, flat piece off a lump of soft paperclay with a cutting wire, as described in Chapter 4 (pp. 46–7). Press down the top of the paperclay with a rolling pin on a flat surface. An easy way to keep the slab from sticking to the moist part of the surface is to flip the soft slab over often (between every two or three rolling passes) and to get in the habit of gently placing the slab down on a dry spot to one side between passes.

Ideally, set the leathersoft paperclay on a plaster surface to harden when it is the right thickness, then leave it until it is totally dry. The underside of the plaster will drain moisture while the top dries in the open air. To get air circulation underneath the plaster, prop it up with a set of blocks or wood rails.

ABOVE: Carol Gaskin and Peter Berry (USA), *Frog Spirit*, 1995. Triptych of paperclay earthenware, low-relief, single-fired. Paper-thin draped leathersoft slabs were added to the flat and dry panels and glaze later applied by airbrush, 1.82 m x 3.05 m x 10 cm (6 ft. x 10 ft. x 4 in.). *Photo: Carol Gaskin.*

RIGHT: Klaus Steindulmuller (Germany), 1993. Set of porcelain paperclay wall panels, larger piece: 102 x 76 cm (40 x 30 in.). Imprint of texture from corrugated cardboard serves as a surface for the painterly application of glazes. *Photo: Rosette Gault.*

ABOVE: Rosette Gault, *Light at the Door,* 2012. Paperclay tiles and panels can be made of translucent porcelain and integrated into paperclay frames. Model for larger window panel in porcelain, size with frame 38 x 20 x 10 cm (15 x 8 x 4 in.). *Photo: Rosette Gault.*

RIGHT: Malin Grumstedt (Sweden), *Gröna Löv (Green Leaves),* 2010. Coloured paperclay porcelain with ceramic inlay, 17 x 17 cm (7 x 7 in.). *Photo: Johanna Norin.*

Though it's fine to start creating texture or addding underglaze or glaze to the new tile while it is drying, resist the temptation to lift it, as this causes stress to the leatherhard paperclay. If you must move it, slide it sideways. It's far more strong and stable for moving, finishing edges and trimming and applying colour when dry.

Interface of painting and sculpture

Paperclay tile and panel work allows ceramic artists to merge painting, sculpture and bas-relief techniques. With paperclay, you have time to work on surface detail for contours, to create illusionary effects.

Using ceramic glaze in a painterly way can be a challenge because fired ceramic glazes can change in colour from how they appeared when first applied. You need experience to master how underglazes and glazes will appear after firing. Artists who devote time to this skill can create illusions by drawing and painting on paperclay panels or murals. The Gaskin and Berry mural (p. 109) is an example of the merging of sculpture and painting, and the wall work of Jeanne Henry (p. 107 and opposite) explores ways to create the illusion of depth and vanishing points, even when the panel or tile is in reality only a few centimetres deep. David Furman's panel, above right, is created in the tromple l'oeil tradition, using glazes instead of paint.

Glazes in the ceramic repetoire offer far more special effects than normal oil or acrylic paint, integrating with the new textures of paperclay and paperclay slips, insertions of glazed work, prints, and every sort of variation imaginable.

Gry Ringset (Norway), *Sound Panels*, 2012. Translucent Limoges porcelain and bone china high-fire paperclay, length: 2 m (6 ft.), width: 36 and 64 cm (14¼ and 25¼ in.). *Photo: by the artist.*

Jeanne Henry (USA), *Abbaye Notre-Dame de Senaque with Lavender Fields*, Provence, France, 2003. Stoneware paperclay, low-relief wall panel, 63.5 x 43 x 6.5 cm (25 x 17 x 2½ in.).

'To convey the illusion of mile distance, depth, perspective, and space between the planes, there must be a careful angle or undercut modelled with the edges detail trimmed. Colours and shadows add to this illusion, as in a painting. I work from a testing palette of over 100 commercially-prepared ceramic stains and natural earth oxides; some I gather from the ground in my travels. Colourants are layered with brush or sponge over dry paperclay. Single-fired to cone 6 reduction.' *Photo: Jeanne Henry.*

10

Surface treatments, finishes and glazes

Like traditional clay, paperclay surfaces and finishes range in look and feel from smooth to rough, in every possible paint or ceramic glaze colour and firing method. The different techniques can be used separately or in combination. Attention to surface texture can begin at the slip stage and carry on through all the moisture stages of paperclay before firing. Layers and textures can be built up, carved or rubbed down. Colours can be worked in, washed over, or wiped off and rubbed, and applied before or after joins are made. Additional coats of colour and glaze can continue to the biqsue-fired paperclay, just as in traditional ceramics.

The subject of surfaces, finishes and colour is huge, so we will just review a few underlying principles that can be adapted for paperclay. Unlike paints, where what you see is what you get, ceramic colourants change in the kiln. The question is how much will they change? I will introduce a simple way to create and customise a reliable and compatible palette of colours, texture and glazes that always matches the paperclay I have and is practical for use in a small studio. This system helps keep costs of glaze colour down, and frees an artist to improvise with single or muliple layerings on wet, leathersoft, dry or bisque paperclay. One can apply a full repertoire of paints and varnishes to a dry paperclay form, but these would not survive a kiln firing. Unfired paperclay finishes will be discussed on pp. 116 and 138.

For glazing and ceramic finishes, there are two skills to master over time. The first is how to control the brush or application tools and the second is how to regulate the viscosity (or water content) of the glaze mixture on the brush or application tool.

A single colour can look different when applied thinly rather than thickly, or in layers under or over textures or other glazes. The skilled artist must coordinate and regulate choices such as the size and shape of brush, sponge, spray or pouring cup, and the amount, type, mix and concentration of colour, as well as adjusting pressure at the point of contact with the clay. This skill is more complex than painting because, unless you are using low-fire china paint, overglaze colour methods, which are more predictable, the colour on the brush will change and melt during the fire. It is challenging and very rewarding when all the factors work in harmony to give you a durable ceramic finish. Persistence, patience and practice are key.

LEFT: Gail Ritchie (USA), *Chair Study*, 2010. Fired paperclay, approximately 51 x 28 x 30.5 cm (20 x11 x 12 in.). *Photo: Gail Ritchie.*

Smooth surfaces

Smooth surfaces are easily achieved by the application of a glossy ceramic glaze. If there is texture under the glaze, some glazes melt down and highlight the texture further; others will fill it in or cover it completely. Earlier in the process a smooth surface can be started when the paperclay is leathersoft by dragging a metal or rubber rib tool across the surface, as you will recall from earlier chapters. Cast paperclay will also give a smooth surface while capturing lots of detail.

Where there are nicks in a dry paperclay surface, scrape them off quickly with the edge of a flexing metal rib or blade, then wipe them down with a damp sponge to soften and trim, as discussed in Chapter 5 (pp. 64–5). If you persist in rubbing dry paperclay with a wet sponge, lint will appear, but this burns off in the fire or can be brushed off when dry. While some artists like this effect of a soft, eroded paperclay surface, the surface can be smoothed by applying a fresh layer of clay or paperclay slip, or by scraping the dry paperclay with a flexible, metal, straight-edge rib or blade.

Some artists want a less glossy, skin-like shine and patina on a matt, non-glazed paperclay porcelain. To get this effect, rub a burnishing tool, such as the backside of a spoon, a smooth rock or a scrap of thin plastic bag over dry paperclay that has been lightly wiped with a damp sponge or brushed with thin coats of terra sigillata between polishings. (Terra sigillata is a very thin clay and water wash over an unfired clay surface that gives a soft shine when rubbed.) If there is a little surface moisture, the rubbing process will flatten the cellulose fibres and seal and compress the tiny clay particles to create a shiny, top layer of paperclay.

Because burnished paperclay surfaces are so tight, they are less water-absorbent than normal dry-stage paperclay, so some glazes won't stick well to them. If you wish to make wet to dry joins on a burnished surface, make sure to re-wet and scratch up joining spots to reopen the surface.

ABOVE LEFT: For a smooth patina, dampen dry paperclay and brush on thin coats of terra sigillata (or just super-thinned paperclay slip). Rub, burnish and buff to a shine in between coats. Rub and compress the dry paperclay surface with a scrap of very thin plastic bag (as shown here), a smooth rock, or the back of a spoon. *Photo: Melissa Grace Miller.*

ABOVE RIGHT: Seeds stick in the wet slip and then dry securely in place. Fill in fresh new layers of slip around the seeds with a brush and clean up any excess with a damp sponge. The result is a fired, translucent surface with delicate seed voids. Work in progress and method by Thérèse LeBrun, (Belgium). *Photo: Paul Gruszow.*

ABOVE LEFT: Linda Saville (USA), 2009. Shreds of coconut fibre were soaked in paperclay slip and modelled. The form was fired and smoked in reduction, raku style. The coconut burned away early on but residues of metallic lustre are visible in the texture. *Photo: Rosette Gault.*

ABOVE RIGHT: Brush paperclay slip over a stencil to build up surface texture on a dry paperclay tile. *Photo: Rosette Gault.*

RIGHT: Thérèse LeBrun (Belgium), Seed pod forms, 2008. Seeds and pressings leave voids after the firing, 30 x 12 cm (11¾ x 4¾ in.). *Photo: Paul Gruszow.*

Integration of surface texture

In Chapter 4, we saw some ways that texture can be started by paddling soft paperclay with a stiff brush or scratching with a needle, fork, comb or serrated rib. Paperclay can be imprinted with rubber stamps, leaves, paperclay stamps and lace, and these textures can be enhanced and built up when the paperclay is dry. For example, you can drag a fan brush dipped in paperclay or non-paperclay casting slip, engobes, underglaze, glaze or paperclay slip across the dry texture to build up layers. Textures built this way can be carved back down with a fettling tool to give crisp edges and borders when dry. For example, the photo on p. 123 shows textures applied by fan brush over dry paperclay. In the same picture we see what a difference changes to firing temperature or recipe can make to the degree of texture.

Paperclay slip adds new possible surface textures to the ceramic repertoire, variously resembling paper, porridge, water, a whirlpool, a river, cresting waves, cake icing, hairy tufts and numerous others. Adjust the amount of water in the paperclay slip to get a thick paste and achieve these effects. You can also make puddles and pools of paperclay slip. High-pulp slip will dry intact without any cracks. For intentional cracking-up textures in drying, reduce the amount of pulp.

To get even more complex textures, artists stir coconut fibre, sawdust, grass, seeds, rice, noodles and other organic combustibles into paperclay slip, again applying the resulting mixture as a thick or thin paste to their chosen surface.

Colours

As mentioned at the beginning of the chapter, ceramic colours derived from minerals are stable and permanent when fired. Although pigments, paints and stains derived from plants will offer colour too, these tend to bleach out or burn away if fired.

Paperclay allows you a choice about whether or not to fire. Some projects do not need the permanence of ceramic, or a kiln is not available nearby. The full measure of paints, oils, acrylics, latex, stains and even shoe polish can be used on paperclay that won't be fired. An unfired surface may need a cover coat that will resist water and moisture and to prepare the surface for painting. Coatings from the marina, auto and building industries, such as polyurethane coating and water-resistant sealant coats, are available.

Ceramic artists, potters and sculptors face the challenge of finding the best possible surface effects to suit their forms. A general principle to bear in mind when thinking about colour is that, for a complex assembled form with lots of detail, you don't need to add too much surface colour. Minimise distractions from the main idea of your work and keep the glaze simple. Conversely, very complex surfaces and painterly effects can be enhanced on a simple geometric form such as a flat panel, plate, box, pot or sphere.

Maria Oriza (Spain), *Pluma*, 2010. Stoneware paperclay with red slip and cobalt oxide, 29 x 65 x 16 cm (11½ x 25½ x 6¼ in.). *Photo: courtesy of Maria Oriza.*

ABOVE: Vary the water content in paperclay slip surface effects. *Photo: Rosette Gault.*

RIGHT: I store my palette of a dozen concentrates of matt engobe colours in capped bottles, and dispense as needed into bowls or cups for mixing and thinning. Thick, they are opaque; thinned with water, they can be semi-transparent. If thinned with a white colour, they get a more pastel tint. For more hues, I can combine them, or apply them in multiple layers to wet, dry or bisque paperclay at any stage before, during or after assembly. Each is made from a simple clay/glaze mixture, which I stain to the maximum with high-fire rated ceramic stain or oxide concentrate. On p. 123 you can see firing test results for the clay/glaze mix. When fired, they are a bit like commercial underglaze. If I need a high-gloss surface, I apply transparent glaze over top. *Photo: Rosette Gault.*

Ceramic glazes and engobes

The full complement of durable, familiar glaze colours and finishes adapts well to paperclay. This includes commerical glazes as well as underglaze slips and engobes, washes of ceramic stain or oxide, which could be worked into the surface by hand before firing, or are more commonly applied by sponge, brush, spray, dipping or pouring over the bisque. Gloss glazes will melt nicely to a smooth, watertight, easy-to-clean surface. Without glaze, paperclay usually fires matt. Test-fire a sample to know what your paperclay and glaze combination will do. Commercial glaze and ceramic engobes are prepared to match base clay bodies, sorted into three firing temperature categories: low-fire (earthenware, terracotta, raku), mid-range or high-fire (porcelain and stoneware).

As dry paperclay is absorbent, it will accept glaze, so single firing can be considered. This means you can apply glaze directly to dry paperclay. If you make a mistake on dry paperclay, clean it with care. You can wipe or scrape glaze mistakes off dry ware, but be careful how much water you are using if the work has thin areas. Single firing is further discussed on pp. 132–3.

The colours and stains for paperclay are as varied as those used for traditional clay. A wide range of firing methods are possible, too, which can give a glassy sheen, depth and lustre. When applied over textured surfaces, the colour of a ceramic glaze can sometimes break into two or more colours – one where thin and another where thick. In addition to the glaze itself, each type of firing gives a different finish, be it oxidation, reduction, wood, gas, electric, raku, salt, soda, saggar, lustre or pit.

With paperclay, I can apply coats of ceramic colour in the form of underglaze, slips, engobe or glaze at any time during the process of making. This allows some simple shortcuts that are not so practical in traditional clay. To get a clean border between colours on two parts, apply underglazes or engobes to the dry parts separately *before* joining them. It's easy to trim up edges and borders when all is dry with a fettling knife, needle or sponge.

ABOVE LEFT: Irit Abba (Israel), *Collection*, 2004. Porcelain paperclay, diameter: 35–40 cm (13¾–15¾ in.). *Photo: Tamar Goldschmidt.*

ABOVE RIGHT: Cynthia Gavião (Brazil), detail from series *Imagem 8*, 2008. Porcelain paperclay. *Photo: Cynthia Gavião.*

RIGHT: Single-fire glazing. Paperclay ware is strong and water-absorbent enough to allow brief dips, sprays or brush applications of ceramic glaze. Works in progress, Jon Williams (USA). *Photo: Rosette Gault.*

Build your palette of ceramic surfaces

An artist will ultimately develop a reliable 'palette' for colour, glaze and surface treatments that is unique to them and compatible with their paperclay. The spectrum of choices is infinite, but many are unpredictable until their application is mastered. Some artists even prefer glaze colours and surfaces to be variable, thriving on the experience of surprise and wonder when they open a kiln. In the ceramic tradition, we rather love the variation in colour we can get in kilns. Changes in kiln atmosphere will affect some colours dramatically; a glaze that appears light copper green when fired in oxidation in an electric kiln may change to red or even give a metallic lustre in a reduction-fired gas or wood kiln, for example.

Others prefer simply to apply ceramic colours in a painterly way and have much more control over the final result, at least at first. If this is the case, make sure to get as much practice as you can in the whole glaze application process to reduce the number of unpredictable variables. Learning to regulate the water content of the glaze will

RIGHT: Stephanie Taylor (USA), *Confluence*, 2011. Paperclay mosaic in progress, each structure approximately 2.75 m x 91.5 cm (9 ft. x 3 ft.) *Photo: Stephanie Taylor.*

BELOW LEFT: Apply colour before, during and after assembly. One artist's challenge was to scale up and transform a flat postcard image into sculpture. To get the illusion of perspective, variations in colour and contour were needed. Underglaze colour was applied to parts before they were joined. Jeanne Henry (USA), work in progress, *Oaxacan Monastery in Mexico*, 46 x 43 x 33 cm (18 x 17 x 13 in.). *Photo: Jeanne Henry.*

BELOW RIGHT: Apply underglaze or glaze to the dry section beforehand. Then join flat tiles dry to dry with a seam of paperclay slip. If need be, trim after the join is dry. Joyce Centofanti (USA), work in progress. *Photo: Joyce Centofanti.*

be key. If you apply glaze on dry paperclay, the surface can be scribed on or scratched with a sharp needle, blade or serrated rib to add even more texture. Edges of colour can be carved in clean lines. When dry, the surface could be stained again with a fresh, thin wash that allows some of the colour underneath to show through. The colour can be set in a bisque or sinter firing. You can make an opaque cover coat over a colour or a section you don't like, or if thinned, show some or all of the colour below. When you want a gloss surface, just brush or dip a fresh coat of transparent glaze over it all to finish, or fire the work to a much hotter temperature to melt the colours down more.

Method overview

Because I need precision with ceramic colour and texture and I want my colours to be compatible with my paperclay, I have worked out a simple method of decoration that involves applying layers of a custom-coloured slip to the paperclay. To finish, I may apply a final transparent, glossy glaze over the matt colour. When I want flashy effects, I use them in combination with stable palette colours: a mixture of both safe and risky approaches to glazing. Nowadays, in many parts of the world, there are reliable commercial underglazes and glazes for sale that will work with paperclay. Alternatively, those who want to gain more understanding of how clay and glazes interact can create their own underglazes.

I vary colour intensity and hue by watering down thick and opaque-coloured slips out of the bottle to get a semi-transparent wash or by mixing different colours together. The colours can be applied to paperclay at any moisture stage, but at dry they allow infinite adjustments and enhancements, the way that paint does. Any colour, once fired, will be set and can't be changed, but unsatisfactory colour application can be touched up or covered completely with a fresh layer from the same colour palette at the bisque stage, or a wash of thinned colour can be sponged over the under-layer and bisque-fired again to see if it has corrected the problem, before the final gloss glaze is applied. A coating of transparent gloss glaze affects the hue of matt underglazes. If you get bisque-fired underglaze wet, the glistening of the water will resemble gloss glaze, giving a little preview!

Most importantly, with this method I can regulate the feel of the surface texture to range between matt, satin matt and gloss. I do this by first making a base mixture of clay and glaze that melts down a little or a lot, depending on what I want. I avoid mess and dust by mixing only wet ingredients in my small studio. I use simple cups instead of scales to measure powders, which saves time.

More often layers of colour are applied, whether paperclay is wet or dry, though it can also be applied after bisque firing for touching up, a cover coat or special effects. One benefit of applying before firing is that after the applied colour is dry, I can detail the dry coat of engobe or glaze with needle or fettle tools to get special texture effects and sgrafitto-like markings.

Process

To mix my own set of underglazes, like those shown in the photo on p. 117, I start with three basic ingredients: clay slip, clear glaze and colourant (sourced from ceramic

The palette of colours can be combined. Here, colours were applied by brush to dry paperclay for a single firing. Underneath the brushwork I applied a white base 'texture' of 50/50 casting slip and clear glaze. After coloured slip was applied, it soaked into the undercoat below and melted with it during firing. If coloured slip is applied first and then a thin white base applied over it, the surface colours fade a bit. A coat of clear gloss glaze will usually brighten the colours below. You can mix and match to get special effects; test various colours to learn your favourites. *Photo: Rosette Gault.*

stain or mineral-oxide powder). For clay, I use either low- or high-fire casting slip, compatible with (or the same as) the base clay used in my paperclay. I mix or buy a clear transparent glaze, which I test to be sure it melts well on my base clay. I stir measures of liquid clay and liquid glaze together to make an all-purpose, white-firing base mix. The more glaze I add proportionally, the more melting and gloss I will see on the surface. Recipes for slip/glaze are explored in the next section, and fired results are demonstrated in the photo on p. 123.

Colour selection and development

The 'base' mixtures usually turn white when fired if white slip was used. To get a new base slip colour, stir in a favourite, suitable ceramic stain. Here is where you can personalise the palette of fired colour to your taste. Check the stain product's fine print (usually stains come as a powder in a small bag) to be sure that it is suitable for a clay firing to your highest temperature. Many will not pass this test.

If you are a beginner, start simple. Even just two colours (a dark and a light tone) can be mixed and matched, and layered thick and thin, to give astonishing variation. Later, add to your palette with a few choices in colour groups: some dark and light hues of blue, green, red, yellow, orange, etc., plus black and white. If desired, mix some of these together to get your own special hue, but keep track of what you test so you can repeat

GLOSS TRANSPARENT CERAMIC GLAZE

CLAY THINNED WITH WATER

Stir some liquid transparent gloss glaze into a casting-slip clay (or light-coloured firing clay thinned with water). Choose a transparent glaze that is compatible with your base clay. The more glaze you add, the more soft and shiny the melted surface will be after the fire. The less you add, the more matt the result. *Photo: Gayle St Luise.*

it. You can also change the desired surface results from matt to smooth to gloss, by changing the proportions of clay to glaze, as seen in the examples in the photo opposite.

Reading the test tiles from top to bottom, we see that the top row (Test 1) is transparent glaze with no clay. The commercial brand, rated to cone 04, looks green when brushed on and green when liquid out of the bottle, as seen in the little cup at the top left of the picture. Some transparent clear glazes look white, others blue. Many but not all commercial glazes will hold up to cone 6 when applied very thinly, although they are not advertised for this. Test yours to see.

In the second row (Test 2) is the volume mixture of 1:1 (half liquid glaze and half liquid slip: Rosette's 50/50). In Tile 2C, the brush texture applied before firing (Tile B) softens a little at cone 04 but melts together completely at cone 6 (2D). In the third row (Test 3) is the mixture of 1:3 (one unit of liquid glaze to three units of liquid slip: Rosette's 1:3). The brushed glazed texture does not melt as much as Test 2 did at cone 04 (3C). Little cracks are showing in places, but at cone 6 the texture has begun the process of fusing and is losing some of its texture detail (3D).

The bottom row (Test 4) is plain, low-fire casting slip with no glaze. You can see that plain casting slip, which looks dark grey in the sample cup on the lower left, can be brushed on with no glaze added. It is dry matt when fired and does not melt very well by itself. When overfired, as in Tile 4D, the surface starts to crack up but other types of over-fired low-fire clay melt to a liquid.

In this chart we get a sense of the full spectrum of melting possibilities from combinations of the all-glaze gloss at the top, down to the matt clay slip at the bottom. This is the principle behind a line blend glaze melt test. Those who want precision beyond what is shown here vary the ratio of clay and glaze in the mix.

Reading down columns B, C and D, we see the changes that occur as the proportion of glaze to clay decreases. Reading across, we can compare changes to the texture and surface when temperature is increased.

Results

Once the simple principle of regulating the glaze melt is grasped, you can fine-tune the result to create a custom look and feel. As you build up layers of depth and/or colour for highlights, your distinctive surfaces will become as unique as your handwriting.

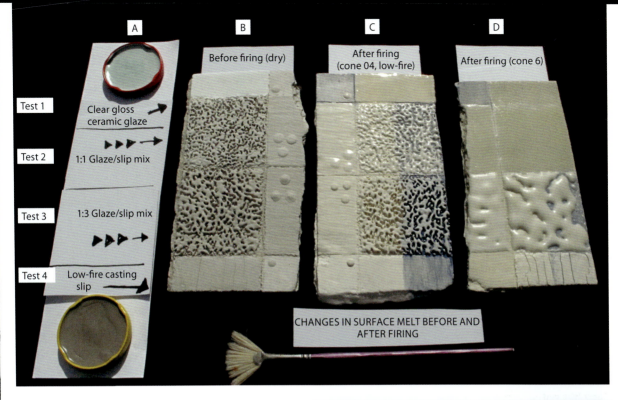

	A	B	C	D
		Before firing (dry)	After firing (cone 04, low-fire)	After firing (cone 6)
Test 1	Clear gloss ceramic glaze ➤			
Test 2	▶▶▶ → 1:1 Glaze/slip mix			
Test 3	1:3 Glaze/slip mix ▶▶▶ →			
Test 4	Low-fire casting slip ➤			

CHANGES IN SURFACE MELT BEFORE AND AFTER FIRING

ABOVE: Clay and glaze, before and after firing. Here I compare mixtures to give you a preview of glaze melt after firing to low fire or mid-range temperatures. Logically, the hotter the temperature, the more the melt. If you want a smoother melt, add more glaze, as in Test 2. If you want a matt surface, reduce the glaze and increase the clay. *Photo: Gayle St Luise.*

RIGHT: Test your colours; they vary all over the world. Preview how your coloured stains will look under or over transparent glazes or engobes by painting the samples in stripes and dots to compare. A glaze coat tends to intensify the colour in some strips, or cause it to go more pastel in others. Raising the firing temperature will also cause a colour shift. Here, the top was fired hotter than the bottom, so you can see how the colours shift from this as well. *Photo: Rosette Gault.*

If you want to increase the degree of melting, add more glaze or increase the firing temperature. To decrease the degree of melting, add less glaze or decrease the firing temperature. This gives you flexibility in many situations. Test some other glaze-to-slip ratios, too (maybe 4:1 or 5:3), as these also work well.

Applying glaze/slip in layers with a fan brush or sponge will build up more effects and textures. A suitable fan brush is shown in the photo above.

The artist who takes the time to understand some of the principles behind ceramic glaze and clay combinations will find many choices of ready- and studio-made glazes to be reliable and compatible with paperclay, particularly when the base clay is similar to or the same as the base slip used in the surface colour and texture treatments, and the clear glaze has been tested and melts well.

11 In the kiln and beyond

Whether oxidation or reduction, high- or low-fire, gas or electric kiln, paperclay fires just like traditional ceramic. The final result will be nearly indistinquishable from traditional ceramic except that it might weigh a little less. The important thing is to find the best temperature for your glazes and base clay. Firing, and the placement and distribution of pots in kilns, is an art in itself. I will touch on just a few key points relevant to paperclay in this chapter, along with the slightly different considerations for large-scale work.

As discussed earlier, paperclay can be left to dry in the open air and force-dried by the application of heat. Before firing, moisture and air travel through paperclay easily via its network of cellulose fibres. Often, after firing, the voids of the cellulose fibre network continue to allow moisture and air to pass through. The point of vitrification and the gradual closure of these pores will vary between base clays. In part because of this, paperclay works can survive a higher degree of temperature change than traditional clay. Paperclay bodies can usually withstand raku and other dramatic firing methods. Paperclay kilns are also popular, but are beyond the scope of this book.

LEFT: Rosette Gault (USA), *Canción de tierra alegría*, 1999. High-fired paperclay porcelain. This photo was taken after eight years outdoors in Seattle's climate of freeze, thaw and rain, 122 x 58.5 x 23 cm (48 x 23 x 9 in.). *Photo: Rosette Gault.*

RIGHT: Julia Nema, *Translucent bowl*, 2004. Porcelain paperclay with Herends porcelain, fired to 1360°C (2480°F). *Photo: Rosette Gault.*

ABOVE LEFT: Paul Chaleff (USA), big pot thrown and assembled in sections, en route to the kiln. *Photo: Paul Chaleff.*

ABOVE RIGHT: **With risky forms (foreground) set like this in a kiln, deformation is likely. Build temporary support for them, just in case. Expect to see evidence of dramatic movement at temperatures close to the fusion temperature of the base clay. Thin porcelain paperclay, rated to cone 10, may be better fired to cone 8. Test-fire it first. To minimise hot spots, distribute the ware and shelves as evenly as possible. Work by students of Julia Nema, Moholy-Nagy University of Art and Design, Budapest.** *Photo: Julia Nema.*

Before firing

For the vast majority of firing methods, work must be totally dry before firing. To avoid creating steam inside clay that is not fully dry, the practice of pre-heating work in the kiln for several hours, at a holding temperature below the boiling point of water, helps ensure the interior of the work is dry before the firing schedule begins and the temperature is raised.

Since I tend to use the non-linear and 'fast dry' methods of assembly, the interior elements are basically dry during most of the later stages of work on the exterior, and may have been dried repeatedly between work sessions, too. This means I am free to use a shorter pre-heat and firing cycle, pre-heating for 2–3 hours or less depending on the size of the work. I prefer relatively high-pulp mixtures, which can withstand a fast firing cycle. If the work is small scale and dry, with thin walls, 2–3 hours should be more than sufficient. If the weather was humid during the making, or if the walls of the piece are thick, then double the time for pre-heating.

If you prefer to follow the traditional 'slow dry' method of leatherhard joins and assembly, the practice is not necessarily safer if the walls of the work are an even thickness. However, if you have any doubt about a damp or wet interior, then do follow a traditional long and low-temperature pre-heating cycle, i.e. overnight for 8–12 hours or more, to be sure the work is truly dry deep inside. Leatherhard paperclay structures enclosed by exterior layers of leatherhard paperclay do take a while to dry completely.

There can be really no precise rule for drying paperclay because of the variations in paperclay mix, user experience and climate. But when the principles of timing the pre-heating and drying process are understood, a better decision can be made.

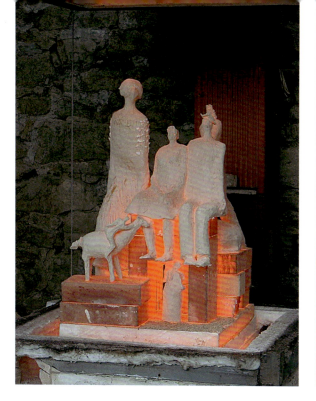

ABOVE, LEFT: Glowing hot stoneware paperclay works-in-progress by Elizabeth Le Retif (France) are exposed to the open air to get special glaze and surface colours, in a variation on raku firing. Red-hot work like this may be moved with long metal tongs and/or thermal gloves. *Photo: Patrick Macé.*

ABOVE, RIGHT: Wali Hawes (India), *Hand, five fingers, five continents*, 2011. Paperclay firing event, with the participation of students from the School of Ceramics, Aubagne, 2.5 x 1.5 m (8¼ x 5 ft.). *Photo: Sylvie Perrotey.*

BELOW: Because paperclay is strong to build with as well as refractory, it can handle thermal shock, so it is also used in fire sculpture events such as Nina Hole's fire towers. The bonfire and firing process is a community event. The public is invited to witness the careful removal and unwrapping of hot blankets of refractory fibre, exposing the glowing sculpture in the form of a red-hot tower. *Photo: Nina Hole.*

Planning a high-temperature firing

Few kilns heat evenly. Both traditional and paperclay forms are likely to soften in thin spots if the kiln gets hotter than planned. Every clay is different, so the only way to know how your paperclay will react is to test it. For firing big sculptures of ungrogged porcelain, place the work in cooler areas and fire to cone 8–9. Common errors will still affect paperclay; for example, errors in the recipe of the base clay or glaze, poor glaze application, poor placement in the kiln, under- or over-firing, carelessness in drying, the ramping up and down of heat and poor design or craftsmanship.

Translucent paperclay porcelain

As the temperature nears the melting point of the base clay, thin-walled porcelain or stoneware can turn soft and glassy for a time. The paperclay structure must withstand the downward pull of gravity during this vulnerable time, which could be 5 minutes or extend for hours in a long wood-firing. Thicker-walled porcelain or stoneware base clays may not soften to this extreme, but thin-walled sections will. Every base porcelain will be translucent if it is thin enough. The right temperature and firing schedule for your particular paperclay porcelain must be learned from experience. A long soaking period at a high temperature may not be best.

Placement in the kiln

Advanced artists find that level kiln shelves make a difference, especially for thin-walled work that will be fired at high temperatures. When the paperclay gets close to a vitreous temperature, thin clay walls begin to soften first. If the temperature is held at a high level and/or reduction atmosphere for many hours, work that stands on an uneven surface may be at risk of deforming. At very high heat, gravity will

BELOW, LEFT AND RIGHT: Thin porcelain figures are at risk of slumping during a high-temperature firing, close to the vitrification point. I improvised some stable props under the arms and nearby to catch or limit movement in the kiln. I have allowed some space between the figure's arms and the props below in case the arms drop a little in firing. If I didn't leave a little space, the propped arm would be held higher while the body of the figure shrunk down, and this new angle and gesture might not be what I want. *Photos: Gayle St Luise.*

Rosette Gault (USA), *Frozen Sun*, 1998. Glazed cone 8 porcelain paperclay in an extreme climate. The outdoor temperature can vary between -40°C (-40°F) in winter and 40°C (104°F) summer. This work was located outdoors in Banff, Canada for over 10 years. The base is wide open inside. *Photo: Rosette Gault.*

slowly but surely cause the work to warp out of balance and move off-centre, no matter what size it is.

If you suspect a thick or exposed section is at risk of drooping in a hot spot, set a stack of bricks as a safeguard a few inches under it, or build a custom paperclay support that is not attached, but which you fire with the work and remove afterwards. See Chapter 8 for armatures, and the next page for information about saggars.

Loading panels and tiles

As a precaution against uneven heat or over-firing, lay paperclay panels or tiles flat in the kiln. Panels could bridge a set of clean and level kiln shelves. For big tiles, I tend to sprinkle a little bit of fine grog on the shelf under each one. I also leave a space of about 10 cm (4 in.) between the panels and the shelf stacked above. Beginners should avoid firing thin slabs or tiles upright and/or on edge due to the risk of uneven heating in the majority of kilns. There are commercial tile-setter frames that could be used, but few artist studios have them on hand.

Loading and fitting multiple-part sculptures

For multiple-part sculptures, the sectioning between the big parts does not need to have been cut in a straight line. In a large stacking figure, a horizontal cut-line between parts distracts the eye, but curved seams between parts may not interrupt the lines of the unified form. There is no requirement for setting big paperclay parts flat on a kiln shelf unless it makes sense for your project. Prop a curved section on the kiln shelf with a firebrick, wadding or shim of kiln clay. Alternatively, you can set an irregular section in a temporary bed of grog or other refractory material, contained in a wide firing bowl of unglazed clay or paperclay that you remove after firing.

Loading kilns with saggars

A saggar is usually a ceramic clay ring or box that protects a delicate pot set inside it. Both are fired together and the pot is removed afterwards. Unglazed lightweight paperclay saggars can be stacked up neatly and loaded in a kiln without disturbing the glaze application on the pot's surface. A saggar protects the pot from debris falling on the glaze before and during firing, but artists also use the inside of a saggar to get special glaze effects. All kinds of combustibles that react with paperclay and/or glaze to give flashing effects and colour can be stuffed inside with the pot, or you can wrap the pots or figures in wire and let the metal react with the clay or glaze (recall safety warnings on pp. 37–8). A saggar keeps all this separate from the other works in the kiln.

The firing process

Like traditional clay, paperclay works will pass through temperature thresholds during firing and cooling and the kiln atmosphere can be oxidation or reduction. Oxidation is common in an electric kiln, while reduction is common in wood, gas, oil, raku and pit firing methods. There are many good books about firing that expand on what is introduced in this chapter. The purpose of this section is to help you understand how paperclay is influenced by temperature changes in the kiln.

The first hour(s) of firing

The most critical temperature to pass safely through in any firing is 100°C (212°F). Expanding pressure from steam is the principle cause of explosions and bursts. As with traditional clay, steam within the clay needs time to escape as the firing process begins. Avoid creating conditions for trapped steam, such as an overly rapid initial heating period. Dry, high-pulp paperclay has many built-in escape routes for steam through its cellulose fibre network. A couple of hours keeping the temperature below 100°C (212°F) will be sufficient if unfired work is thoroughly dry and has been through a pre-heating period also. Allow more time in a humid climate.

Paper and organic material burn-out time at 253°C (451°F)

The low-temperature burn-out of wax resist and cellulose fibre is about the same. Both will smoke for a few hours at this temperature (which will be reached soon after the steam escapes). Vent the kiln and tell your neighbours they might smell some paper or wax burning until you know how well your ventilation system works. Without a kiln vent, I leave peep-holes or the lid open a fraction until the smoking process is finished; that should take two to three hours maximum. The kiln temperature is still far too cool for this type of smoke to damage the heating elements in an electric kiln. To put this in perspective, the total amount of pulp in a kiln full of paperclay is still much less than, for example, the crumpled paper 'stuffing' some artists use inside soft clay forms when hand-building. People fire this all the time without a second thought.

Labels in image, left to right:
Texture glaze on paperclay
Hollow interior fired dipped bird nest
No grog No sand No chamotte Thick paperclay with glaze
Wood-fired Thick and thin Limoges porcelain paperclay
Perlite paperclay (thick)
Perlite
'Sinter fired' paperclay

Curio cabinet of fired paperclays. From left to right: a very thick, fired texture applied in layers by fan brush; a bird's nest dipped in paperclay slip and then fired (you can see the twigs left inside); 5 cm (2 in.) thick, solid, high-pulp earthenware; 3 cm (1¼ in.) thick wood-fired porcelain tile with a carved and modelled 'stairway' leading to a thin section in the deepest part, only 3 mm; a lightweight chunk of porcelain paperclay with perlite, fired; front and centre: carving details on sinter-fired paperclay with a fettling tool.
Photo: Gayle St Luise.

If your paperclay contains organic additions, intended to create special texture, Luca Tripaldi suggests holding the heat at 315°C (600°F), slower than normal for paperclay, with very thick work held at this stage for as long as six hours, before resuming a normal paperclay firing schedule.

Sinter firing and/or low bisque for carving

A sinter firing to about 480–540°C (900–1000°F) takes only a few hours. This is just below or near the quartz-inversion temperature (573°C/1063°F, or less than cone 022). The result will be an open, soft but stable surface that resembles soapstone or soft plaster. The texture is smooth to carve and the crisp edges of a non-grog-bearing paperclay are impeccable without any fibre. To reduce dust when carving, soak the paperclay wet first. Place a damp towel below to catch dust from carving.

Bisque firing

When the kiln is red hot inside, glazes for earthenwares and raku start to melt. This is also the temperature range for bisque firing. If a bisque (intermediate) firing is planned for glaze application, fire to cone 03 or 04. At low-temperature bisque, around cone 08, earthenware paperclays might be OK, but most high-pulp and high-firing stoneware or porcelain paperclay will be too fragile and will need a higher temperature. The trade-off is that at cone 08 many porcelain and stoneware paperclays are also soft enough to carve on. Paperclay bisque will accept paperclay slip, so can be integrated with assemblies of unfired paperclay and then re-fired, and can sometimes be patched (see pp. 32 and 78).

The fire is started with kindling on a bed of hot coals. The wet pieces are nearby, but they will 'toast' dry if turned. Eventually, very dry and hot pots can be nudged into the coals with a stick. When pots are red hot, they can be removed, or dug out of the ashes the next day. *Photo: Rosette Gault.*

Loading dry sculpture into the kiln for a single high-temperature firing. Gloss glaze was applied to the interior surfaces before the exterior sides were assembled and sealed as one. Exterior surface finish was applied also. Porcelain work in progress by the author. *Photo: Donald Lee.*

Clay bodies in a reduction firing

If you have a reduction atmosphere kiln, there are more variables to consider. Since paper burns out so early on in the firing process, it is long gone before the glazes melt. In raku firing, and for advanced methods involving thermal shock, paperclays perform well. Some celadon glazes may see a slight colour shift. To create or avoid a carbon trapping effect during reduction firing, change the rate of heating and cooling in the kiln. Carbon trapping can occur when a glaze melts and seals clay prematurely. It can give a dark hue or smoky soft 'clouds' under what might otherwise be an opaque or clear glaze.

Single firing

With paperclay, bisque firing is optional because dry paperclay is sturdy and water-absorbent enough to withstand the glazing processes. However, if you make a mistake in applying the glaze, correcting it may require some extra steps. Thin-walled dry paperclay can become waterlogged and start to soften, so wait for glaze to dry between applications (though glaze can be washed off a bisque-fired piece under running water). Test your glazes and surface treatments first to see if they will work in a single firing. In Chapter 10, I discuss glazes and surface treatments, and explain some more methods with slips and engobes, compatible with single firing.

Another more primitive method for high-pulp paperclay (and not traditional clay) is firing in an open flame. This variation on pit firing and raku works with small works. Pieces are 'toasted' dry by pre-heating and rotating close to the heat every 15–20 minutes (as you might do at barbeque, to get all the sides cooked!). Surface burnishing and simple colours are added when dry or wet, before the pre-heating begins (see also p. 114). The pots are moved closer to the fire in gradual increments of time and distance. Finally, they can be nudged into, and eventually under, the coals in the fire.

After a while, the pots will glow red, as in a raku firing. They can be left in the fire and ash to cool, or withdrawn with tongs and gloves and treated much the same as a raku pot might be for effects. They can be smoked and doused in lukewarm water, or buried in sand or ashes, to cool them quickly. If pursuing this method, wear eye protection, leather gloves and protective natural-fibre clothing, and supervise others around the fire. Try extreme firing methods like this at your own risk: there are far too many variables for the author or publisher of this book to guarantee your safety.

Multiple firings

Just like traditional clay, paperclay allows multiple firings. Since cellulose fibre burns away during the first firing, only ceramic remains for glazes and firings thereafter. Traditional ceramic methods all carry over; you can fire the same project many times to different temperatures for layering glazes and achieving different surface effects.

Vitrification and firing limits

In some high-pulp paperclay, the precise vitrification temperature could shift by a cone or more. Tensile strength could also change. Fire a paperclay sample a few cones down (for high-fire, high-pulp paperclay) or up (for low-fire, high-pulp). Alternatively, adjust the amount of flux in the clay recipe, to reduce or increase the openness of the body and/or compensate for unknown amounts of clay in the paper recipe. Some porcelain bodies in a reduction atmosphere could change to a tan colour due to trace irons or other metals in recycled paper ink that is not based on vegetable oil.

Thin, fired paperclay porcelain can be as brittle as an eggshell. Paperclay that is under-fired, immature, in which the base-clay recipe is poor, or that has too much grog or sand in it, could crumble in your hand. Some, when fired to maturity, have sharp edges like glass if shattered.

Stephanie Taylor (USA), *Floating Buoy*, 2008. The artist sets one of her glazed paperclay orbs to float in her garden pond, diameter: approx. 30.5 cm (12 in.). *Photo: Rosette Gault.*

Paperclay and glass

Methods of glass firing carry over for paperclay. As glass and paperclay are compatible, there have been many artists exploring this from both technical and conceptual directions. Artists have integrated melted glass in boxes filled with glazed paperclay figures in multiple firings. Paperclay can also serve as a mould in which to melt glass, as a frame for slumping. Anne Turn (see opposite) combines both glass and paperclay porcelain and fires them in ensemble.

What not to fire

I discourage firing paperclay-dipped metals in any school settings because of the fumes (see also pp. 37–8). Dipped foam rubber, Styrofoam, sponges, plastic bags, cups and other plastics will generate a thick, black smoke that has nothing to do with the paper and everything to do with man-made materials, generating unhealthy airborne VOCs (volatile organic compounds). As it is, the burn-out of dipped organic materials like thick, solid wood can generate small amounts of gases or smoke, in addition to normal burn-out gases and airborne sulphuric compounds of clay, which are not healthy to breathe in an enclosed space like a studio for long periods of time. Always ensure your kiln is well-ventilated.

Be aware that not all 'recycled' paper is the same. In recipes, I discourage adding recycled paper pulp that has flame retardant added to it (see pp. 23, 145, 152). In North America and some other countries, boric acid and other flame retardants are added to building materials, including bags of so-called dry fluff recycled paper, by law. These will generate toxic and foul-smelling smoke for almost the full duration of the firing. Many artists also combine man-made fibres with paperclays, but there is no guarantee what kind of fumes issue from these.

ABOVE: Anne Turn (Estonia), *Ice and Snow*, 1994. The artist combines Egyptian paste with paper, in some cases even at ratios of 1:1. After firing this at 1200°C (2192°F), the piece is used as a mould for melting glass on and through, at 840°C (1544°F). Due to similarity with the composition of glass, and some flexibility thanks to paper, this material keeps glass from breaking and allows the two mediums to cooperate. Dimensions: 10 x 20 cm (4 x 8 in.). *Photo: Anne Turn.*

RIGHT: Horvath Laszlo (Hungary), *Lantern*, 2004. Translucent porcelain paperclay-slip lantern, height: 45.5 cm (18 in.). *Photo: Rosette Gault.*

Visions emerge

As we come to the end of this book, the spirit of expressive freedom embodied in paperclay should by now be evident. In my own art practice, I, like others, sought a means in ceramic to integrate both sculpture and painting, to scale up and express fresh views of the human condition, and after 20 years of trial and error, I discovered a way to do this. I created a set of optimum paperclay recipes that enabled me to build any form I could imagine and overcome almost every technical limitation of traditional ceramics. I gained the freedom to assemble and build forms of ceramic sculpture by means of an improvisational, non-linear process, which I had yearned for since I first touched clay, and was technically impossible with traditional clay bodies and practices.

There was a time when aspects of the medium, such as the use of paperclay for patch repairs, wet-to-dry joins, dipping and special recipes were unknown outside my studio, but artists could see that what I was doing was impossible with traditional clay. Many questions followed and, when teaching, I urged artists to join me in the testing and research efforts that would be needed. Many clays from across the world have now been mixed into a ceramic paperclay version and fired successfully in a wide variety of kilns. Today, thousands of artists have adapted paperclay in imaginative ways, a new field has opened up and a wide variety of practices have evolved. Paperclay has found a firm place in artists' studios the world over.

The spirit of exploration, delight and wonder I felt has evidently been contagious. As a result of all this synergy, a paperclay knowledge base is now accessible and available to serve the collective imagination in the future. The knowledge base grows with each new teacher and artist adding to it. I am so grateful for all the people in front of and behind the scenes who supported and encouraged us to advance. We have accessed new realms of imagination and awareness that have grown over time to the point where my long-held vision for a panoramic book like this could at last be written and find its way to you.

LEFT: Annika Teder (Estonia), *The Corals*, 2011. These larger-than-life forms are fired to porcelain temperatures in a kiln and then assembled. Porcelain paperclay, 3 x 3 m (10 x 10 ft.) *Photo: Annika Teder.*

RIGHT: Marcia Selsor (USA), *Sketches of Spain: Marking the Millennium*, 1998. Installation at the Yellowstone Art Museum, Billings, Montana. *Photo: Marcia Selsor.*

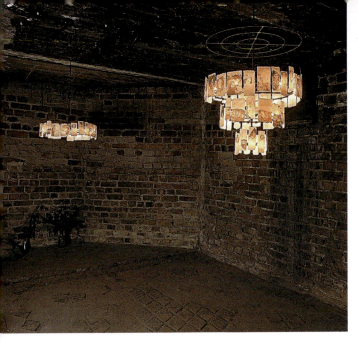

Maarit Makela (Finland), *Chandeliers*, 2006. High-fired and translucent paperclay porcelain, glazed photo-screen images. *Photo: Rauno Traskelin.*

Artist collaboration coordinated by Gurdrun Klix (Germany), *Hinter den Mauern (Behind the Walls)*, 1998. Paperclay. *Photo: courtesy of the artist.*

Unfired paperclay

Any size of paperclay can be finished without firing – as large as doors and transport vehicles permit. Further changes in size, shape or weight are unlikely, as dry paperclay has finished shrinking. Temporary forms built, for example, for a theatre or dance set, could be deconstructed after the show, slaked down and reused.

Sheltered works will keep indefinitely in a dry location. Unsheltered works are vulnerable to weathering, and rain and snow will slowly erode the surface. Over time, colours in unfired works may fade in sunlight, or the finish could dull, break down or peel off during cleaning. The cleaning and maintenance of large work needs to be part of the plan. Even indoors, the top of the sculpture where dust falls will need to be wiped clean periodically.

It could be that a work is built for a kiln that is not nearby, or that a kiln large enough to fire the work becomes available years after the work was made. Maybe the work is coated with paint or varnish in the meantime and has been placed indoors for a long while. If a paperclay work is coated with paints and left unfired, then fired later on, the paints will burn away.

Cover coats and sealants for unfired paperclay include most artists' and sculptors' media, such as pigments, stains, oil, acrylic, tempera, glue thinned with water, paints, wax, encaustics, varnish, resins, fibreglass and polyurethane. Paints and coatings from the marine, auto, and construction industries can seal over paperclay, too. Polish and shine over any of these air-setting media, just as you would normally. Plain, burnished paperclay (see p. 114) can sometimes be enough. Note that chalks and pastels may be easier to apply to a bisque surface.

Laura Palazzi Von Buren (Venezuela), *Entreverde*, 2010. Paperclay and mixed media, 1.5 m x 1.5 m x 7 cm (5 ft. x 5 ft. x 2¾ in.). *Photo: Felipe Figuera Villanueva.*

Installation

Temporary installations with both fired and unfired paperclay are very popular. Dry paperclay is strong enough to set up anywhere. Where indoor space is not practical, outdoor space may be possible.

Many artists like the idea of deconstructing/constructing a work before, during and after a show. Often they don't save or store the paperclay work; rather, they reclaim it. Though they could save the work, many of them ask, 'Why?' and 'Where?' and 'Who for?', and also, 'How long will I have to pay storage fees on a work that was like a theatre event but is now history?' Instead, they slake the dry paperclay elements back down in water and start a new project. In these cases, there is no physical object left after the show for a patron to collect or trade, except perhaps a photo or fragment of the deconstructed work as a memento; if it is a fired work, the artist might take a hammer to it and save a few pieces. The physical work may be ephemeral, but the photo documentation lives on after the show is over. This is a challenging idea for those who value art and ceramic art as a medium that will outlast painting.

As can be seen in a few instances with unfired paperclay in this chapter, we observe an interaction between art and its environment that can be beautiful and telling. To offer one example, we get a vicarious experience of watching snow and weather consume the seat of Lauren Mayer's paperclay chair, shown in the sequence overleaf. The effect of a freeze-thaw cycle does not change the unfired sculpture all at once. We can predict a collapse but we can't know when or how it will change or lose form.

In this work we see indirect reference to the Situationist school of art, events and objects from the 1950s and 60s. The Situationists set up spontaneous and ephemeral events that gave viewers a chance to notice everyday occurrences from a new point of view.

Everything from moss and grass to seeds can be mixed into porous paperclay, just as they can with traditional clay, to create potentially otherworldly forms of topiary. Seeds can take root and burst a paperclay form open. Graham Hay reports that bright yellow lichen started to grow on the sides of one of his unfired outdoor installations in Australia.

Also popular are budget-friendly, low-cost, ready-made objects reclaimed from secondhand stores, which can easily be combined, dipped or fused with paperclay, whether fired or not. Linda Sormin's (USA) installations use large assemblies of fired and unfired paperclay with other media. They seem a whirlwind of debris at first sight, but as half of the installation is airborne, or nearly so, it is possible to walk inside it and get a direct experience as well.

K.C. Adams (Canada) has created remote-controlled porcelain paperclay sculptures. Motion-sensitive hardware is fitted inside and the presence of a viewer causes the sculpture to twitch and move. Shelly Wattenbarger has built exotic paperclay housing for tiny animated movies (p. 142); you must look inside the work to see the projected animations within. Mark Nathan Stafford has built steam-producing apparatus into his figures; steam from a container of hot water hidden inside will periodically exit in puffs through the eyes and the ears of one of his life-sized figures (see p. 82).

In some countries, Denmark, Israel and Mexico among them, artists have projected theatre lights, animations and videos onto paperclay sculptures to give the impression of a dynamic surface. Twenty years ago, as an alternative to glaze, Brian Gartside (New Zealand) taught a similar idea, projecting colourful images from a slide projector onto his sculptures during workshops. With today's digital technology artists can easily project colour images and movies onto paperclay in installations.

Sometimes it seems as if airborne installation has become its own genre; it is popular because paperclay is lightweight. Gudrun Klix (Germany) and a team of helpers pressed soft paperclay onto a brick wall at a former hospital. When the panels had set hard enough to release from the wall, a surface impression of the masonry texture was left on the back. These imprints of the wall's texture were suspended like sheets, swaying gently at eye level in mid-air. Allen Chen created a line of airborne glazed and fired paperclay structures that show a sequence of metamorphosis, as if part of a 3D-animated storyboard (see p. 101). Artists like Neil Forrest and others toy with scale and space; on p. 75, we see overblown pot shards as airborne fragments of

SEQUENCE, LEFT TO RIGHT: Lauren Mayer (USA), *The Vertigo of Between*, 2010. This work is an unfired chair, cast with paperclay porcelain slip. Over the course of two months at Anderson Ranch Arts Center, this piece was exposed to the elements. It slowly slaked back into the ground. *Photo: Lauren Mayer.*

ABOVE LEFT: Malene Pedersen (Denmark) in collaboration with Veronica Thorseth, *Northern Beach*, 2008. A mobile unfired paperclay vehicle roams the beach Mixed-media event with paperclay structures. *Photo: Malene Pedersen.*

ABOVE RIGHT: Malene Pedersen (Denmark), installation collaboration with Sabine Popp, *Voyage to Inner Space*, 2009. *Photo: Malene Pedersen.*

laminate earth, dangling before us like bait on the line, just out of reach.

We get chances to see the world in new ways as a result of these kinds of projects. Compared to the cost of some art materials, paperclay is affordable and accessible, which has opened the medium up to a more diverse group of people, including artists who have no prior experience in ceramics. They are using paperclay in mixed-media projects and sculpture, unaware of the old caveats of traditional ceramics.

Artists working in traditional clay know that repair to dried work is not possible. Cracks at that stage cannot be patched. Soft slabs tear or collapse when being picked up. Pulling clay out of moulds takes care and perfect timing. Dry work is very fragile; if a handle falls off a dry cup, the project has to be started over. Pots can explode in the kiln and glazes don't turn out as intended. Whole kilns and months of work might be lost. The learning curve in this medium is very steep and for most people the traditional discipline takes years to master.

Artists with minimal experience in the ceramic discipline can construct paperclay forms without prejudice or fear of cracks or loss, unaware that such a form in traditional clay would not survive. The visual result has stimulated the imagination

of clay workers the world over, no matter what practice they use. Some wizards who know traditional clay well cannot help but be baffled by the sight of strange new paperclay forms. Indeed, the appearance of these 'wild' forms has opened up a lively dialogue among ceramic artists. A synthesis of mixed media and sculpture with ceramic practice is underway:

> With fired paperclay ... the earthen heaviness of ceramics is lost ... allowing ceramics to become an unrestricted reservoir of personal ideas, dreams and inspirations ... In the exhibition of the International Festival of Postmodern Ceramics (2009), we thereby recognise the transition to the predominant contemporary ceramic expressive approach.
>
> Bernd Pfannkuche, Editor, *New Ceramics Magazine*, Germany – review of the International Festival of Postmodern Ceramics, Varaždin, Croatia, 2009.

On the horizon

In the future, the gaps between sculpture and ceramics will narrow even further. Paperclay has affinities with so many organic and man-made materials that I expect to see many paperclay hybrids and composites with special attributes: extreme hardness, tensile strength, softness, porosity, solubility, refractory, and so on. In due course, as engineers and scientists research the medium, it is likely that the 'alternative' methods of creation in this book will extend beyond the field of ceramic art to other disciplines, too. Paperclay practice offers cost savings, streamlining of

TOP LEFT: Ayala Sol Friedman (Israel), *Pulses*, 2011. "In my objects I work with an action and material. A simple action, monotonous, that repeats itself over and over again in an obsessive, internal rhythm." Hand-built coloured porcelain paperclay, height: 38 cm (15 in.). *Photo: Sasha Flit.*

TOP RIGHT: Antonella Cimatti (Italy), *Tricoloure*, 2011. Paperclay porcelain mounted on glass base, height: 36 cm (14 in.). *Photo: Raffaele Tassinari.*

RIGHT: Karen Harsbo (Denmark), *Farvede søjler 11 (Coloured colums 11)*, 2010. Paperclay, pulp plaster, sandcast, 45 x 30 x 12 cm (17¾ x 12 x 4¾ in.). *Photo: Ole Akhoj.*

production and design, and use with eco-sustainable materials: real opportunities for the products of tomorrow. The task of making paperclay – the material and methods – accessible to the world and laying a practical foundation for its further development has been a life's work.

Artists and designers of all ages and times have striven to create something tangible and beautiful, from nothing but a thought, feeling, or vision. We have witnessed the practical genesis of paperclay forms using creation practices that are impossible with traditional clay. For artists, this is a dynamic modelling medium that serves the imagination like no other.

Appendices

1: Precautions for paperclay

Although every effort has been made to provide accurate and complete information, there are too many variables involving safety precautions, health, fired results, prior experience and so on, to make a guarantee of any kind regarding paperclay. Always test-fire samples of your paperclay in advance. Though the pulps used in P'Clay® and P'Slip® have tested safe and non-toxic in the lab, it is impossible to guarantee untested papers that might be used in an art studio. Health information on risks, allergies and precautions can be found at www.paperclayart.com/151Safety2.html.

Since the author and publisher cannot be held responsible for the consequences of your use of paperclay, use it at your own risk. Please contact the publisher if errors are found that can be corrected in future editions.

Handling safety

Some people are sensitive to minerals or other ingredients in clay or paperclay; a few wear gloves when working with it. Test a sample first to check. Avoid adding bleach to any paperclay batch. Anyone with a known allergy to moulds and mildews should only mix and use fresh paperclay.

In general, avoid storing wet paperclay. Over time, microbial colonies grow in moist conditions in all aged clays, including paperclays. Colonies of microscopic organisms like fungi and bacteria grow slowest in porcelain-based paperclays made with non-inked paper pulp. In a cool environment, these can take many months or years to grow. Paperclays that contain inked, recycled paper pulp

grow microbes very quickly. When these combine with base clays already known for high organic content – such as certain ball clays or terracottas – in warm conditions, visible signs and smells of microbial activity show up in a matter of weeks. The remedy is to dry out flattened scraps of paperclay and then reconstitute it by slaking down in a bucket of water when you're ready to resume work.

Some, but not all, commercially-prepared paperclays have added preservatives.

About firing paperclay

All clays and glaze materials release gases during firing. Good ventilation of the kiln and surrounding area is needed. Most kiln vents or exhaust fans are designed to handle paperclay. The burn-off of paper from natural cellulose fibre is comparable to the burn-off of wax resist and is over within the first few hours of heating. If you have a large kiln-load of high-pulp paperclay, it is courteous to warn neighbours that the smell will end after a few hours.

Avoid firing sources of cellulose fibre that have been pre-treated with fire or flame-retardants. If these are mixed in paperclay, then the smoking period and fumes from these additives can last for 12 hours or more.

Do not fire metals or plastics in kilns near urban areas, offices or schools. Fumes from these are toxic. The residue from some metals can damage nearby ware or the interior of a kiln. Fire only with saggar pots, in rural regions, with excellent ventilation.

2: Firing guide

The firing schedule below is similar to that of traditional ceramic. With experience, the firing time can be reduced. Firing times will vary due to:
1. age and condition of your heating elements and fuel;
2. dryness and thickness of sculpture or ware in kiln;
3. amount of ware in kiln, size of kiln;
4. moisture in atmosphere;
5. ventilation in kiln.

	Room temp	Boiling of water → steam	Paper/wax-resist burn out	Smoking stops	Red heat and higher	Finish temp.
Events inside the kiln	68°F ⇨ ⇨	212°F	451°F	⇨ ⇨	⇨ ⇨	⇨ ⇨ off
Temperature	20°C	100°C ⇨	232°C ⇨			
Time elapsed since ignition	Start	1–2 hours	3–4 hours	⇨ ⇨	6–8 hours	⇨ ⇨
Kiln controls	Lowest heat about 2 hours		Medium about 2 hours	Full power		➡ off ➡ off
Ventilation (manual)	➡ ➡	Door/lid open Peep holes open		Door/lid closed Peep holes closed	➡ ➡	➡ off ➡

Most air-dried paperclay can have a pre-heat/drying time at a temperature below the boiling point of water (90°C/200°F), so steam has time to escape. More than four hours of pre-heating is a waste of power and in dry climates less than two hours is normal. I often use the auto 'fast fire' firing schedule after pre-heating, even for big works. Soak or hold the temperature only if glazes require time to melt smoothly or for crystals to grow. Oxidation and reduction kilns will vary. Always test-fire a sample first to verify likely results. Most paperclay does not need an extreme, slow cool-down. Wait for ware to cool to unload, so work can be handled safely.

3: Recycled papers

Some sources of natural cellulose fibre *(Whitney/Gault 1992)*

Approximate composition	Cotton linter	Linen-flax	'Soft' woods	'Hard' woods
Cellulose $C_6H_6O_5$	96%	85%	50%	50%
Hemi-cellulose $C_{12}H_{23}O_{11}$	3%	10%	20%	30%
Lignins	1%	5%	30%	20%
Note: Pulp break-down timing for each type varies. Papers may need multiple episodes of agitation in hot water and straining to separate fibres into pulp.	Most water-absorbent and fluffy		Soft wood pulp has thinner cell walls than hard wood, so they collapse more quickly when beaten into pulp	The thicker cell walls of wood pulps are sturdier, so they take longer to beat or break apart into pulp. Least absorbent.

3: Recycled papers, continued

Good paper sources	Paper description
Offices, schools	Cotton, linen, flax writing paper or bond
Publishers, printers, letterpress, book pages	Uncoated. Choose non-gloss or matt because the gloss will take a long time to turn into pulp. Book stock, out of date brochures (most ink residues burn off during firing).
Artist studios	Trimmings, drawing papers. Cold press takes less time to turn into pulp than hot press.
Copy centres	Non-gloss copy paper; ink, colours OK. Laser papers with long fibres take more time to turn to pulp.
Computers	Lower-grade laser and copy papers. Tractor feed multiple copy carbons can be pulped together.
Newsprint	Newsprint without plastic varnish over the inks. Most gloss-coated advertising inserts (colour can take more time to break down into pulp).
Household	Egg cartons, toilet paper. Toilet paper disperses quickly when agitated in cold water. (All others in this table need warm or hot to speed the break-down process.)
Avoid	Vellums, gloss-coated paper, window envelopes, staples, adhesive tape, paperclips, rubber bands, cellophane. Sharp items will contaminate a smooth paperclay and may discolour it during firing. Avoid paper towels and facial tissue as these take a long time to turn to pulp. Beware glues used to laminate cardboard boxes, which are difficult to convert back to pulp.

4: Influences on pulp break-down times

Tear test: tear a strip of the paper you want to recycle	Cellulose fibres' relative length	Time needed to break down pulp with hot water and tools
Easy to tear	Short	1 (toilet paper) to 20 minutes, average 5 to 10 minutes. The easiest option.
More difficult to tear	Medium	10 minutes 2 hours beating 'pulp soup' to disperse fibres
Difficult to tear	Long	Mixing for many hours or overnight, multiple straining and remixing required

To speed break-down time:

1. Use plenty of hot water when mixing, the more the better.
2. Have papers shredded and sorted first.

3. Test-fire a small sample of paperclay, as some inks and papers can lend a tan colour to the base clay.

5: Wet to dry adhesion

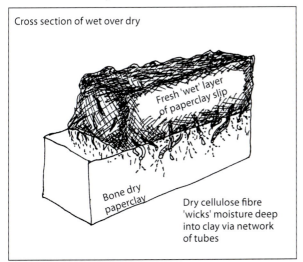

Cross section of wet over dry

Fresh 'wet' layer of paperclay slip

Bone dry paperclay

Dry cellulose fibre 'wicks' moisture deep into clay via network of tubes

6: Repair to dry paperclay

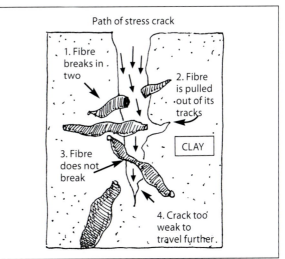

Path of stress crack

1. Fibre breaks in two

2. Fibre is pulled out of its tracks

3. Fibre does not break

CLAY

4. Crack too weak to travel further.

A process of osmosis drags the wet tip-ends of fibres in paperclay slip down into the pores of dry paperclay. Dry cellulose fibre wicks moisture deep into the clay via its network of tubes. Paperclay slip hardens and shrinks in place as it dries. Joins will continue to tighten and strengthen during firing.

The path of a stress crack in dry paperclay is interrupted by fibres along the way. To repair a crack like this, apply a fresh coating of paperclay slip. Moisture will be absorbed into the dry crack and the new patch will shrink in place as it hardens and dries. After the repair, the filled crack will contain a more complex layering of cellulose fibre and clay than before.

7: Comparing ratios of paper pulp to base clay

As seen in the photo on p. 26, use the same-size container to measure ingredients for any size of batch, type of pulp or type of paperclay slip. The ratio measurements do not have to be precise and many artists adapt these rough guides. The five types described here have the different features an artist might require. All can be combined in the same project, especially if the base clays are compatibe.

Ratio of 1 pulp: 1 clay (paperclay light)

This mix looks and feels very papery; it is not my usual first choice. It is best used when a light fired weight is desired. It is short and not very plastic to model with, but if thinned with water and poured it will pick up the details in plaster well. This mix can be used as thick paste or soft clay, to contour over a dry section, to cast, to model, or to fill in gaps. It can be formed into a solid dry

chunk to carve on or chisel down. Porcelain paperclay mixed at this ratio, when fired, can resemble a smooth, glazed pumice rock, as seen in the photo on p. 131. If this paperclay mix is under-fired, or the base clay contains too much grog or sand, the fired result can be crumbly.

Test your specific clay. If you need a watertight paperclay, adjust the amount of flux in the clay body. Those wanting porous paperclay (for water filtration or another application) might start with this recipe type and fine-tune it by variations in firing temperature and pulp content.

Ratio of 1 pulp: 2 clay (high-pulp)

Particularly suited to big wall panels and larger-scale projects, this high-pulp mix is lightweight when fired. The papery surface can be smoothed down with a rubber rib when leathersoft. Another way to smooth the surface

0011 15KV   X50 100µm WD37

Paperclay, high-pulp, dry. Natural cellulose fibre varies in length and diameter. The rough texture of white fuzz on each fibre suggests the presence of 'nano-fibres', barely visible with the tools available in 1993, when these images were taken. Fibres are loosely aligned because I combed through the paperclay slip (see p. 33).

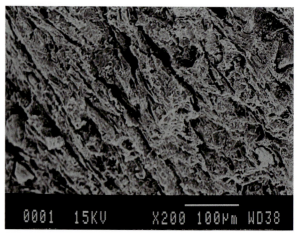

0001 15KV   X200 100µm WD38

Paperclay, high-pulp, fired to 700°C (1292°F). Despite the high-pulp content of the sample, plenty of clay remains after the fibre has burned away. The volume measure was near 1 pulp: 2 clay for this test. The base clay was a low-fire ball clay casting slip, with pulp sourced direct from a a paper mill.

These micrographs are excerpted from the Rosette Gault and David Kingery Testing of 1992 and performed at the University of Arizona. Results were presented at NCECA San Diego Conference, March 1993.

texture is to apply a fresh coat of paperclay slip after it is totally dry. It is a more porous and open paperclay when fired and can be used for casting, as gap filler, or for contour modelling. To optimise the degree of fired strength, porosity or other attributes, bring the firing temperature up a few cones for an earthenware base, or down a few cones for high-fire porcelain, or adjust the amount of flux in the clay body.

Ratio of 1 pulp: 3 clay (all-purpose sculpture)

To get seamless wet-to-dry joins and repairs, use close to a 1:3 ratio, or higher in non-grog, non-grit base like porcelain. The more pulp used, the less surface cracking will occur in patch and dry assembly. This ratio is in the range of my usual mix for large sculptures: the larger the sculpture, the higher the pulp to clay ratio. To fine-

tune the recipe further, consider changing the flux in the clay body recipe or shifting the firing temperature slightly.

Ratio of 1 pulp: 4 clay (low)

This is a mix at the low end of the functional range. In practice it means that repairs to drying cracks need to be patched and repaired more than once.

Ratio of 1 pulp: 5 or more clay (potter's)

This mix is suitable for use on a potter's wheel and for some casting purposes. It is better for small-scale projects. Less fibre means it had best be trimmed and worked in the familiar leatherhard assembly methods, using the linear approach. This mix is more clay-like and vulnerable. Wet-to-dry joins may have to be repaired more than once.

8: Cellulose and synthetic fibre compared

Natural cellulose

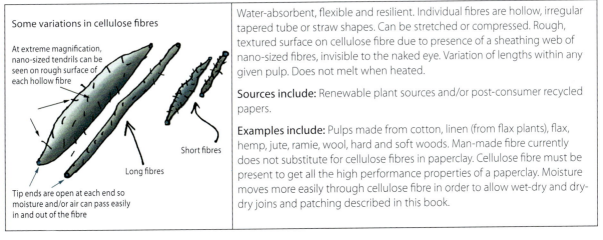

Some variations in cellulose fibres

At extreme magnification, nano-sized tendrils can be seen on rough surface of each hollow fibre

Short fibres

Long fibres

Tip ends are open at each end so moisture and/or air can pass easily in and out of the fibre

Water-absorbent, flexible and resilient. Individual fibres are hollow, irregular tapered tube or straw shapes. Can be stretched or compressed. Rough, textured surface on cellulose fibre due to presence of a sheathing web of nano-sized fibres, invisible to the naked eye. Variation of lengths within any given pulp. Does not melt when heated.

Sources include: Renewable plant sources and/or post-consumer recycled papers.

Examples include: Pulps made from cotton, linen (from flax plants), flax, hemp, jute, ramie, wool, hard and soft woods. Man-made fibre currently does not substitute for cellulose fibres in paperclay. Cellulose fibre must be present to get all the high performance properties of a paperclay. Moisture moves more easily through cellulose fibre in order to allow wet-dry and dry-dry joins and patching described in this book.

Synthetic fibres

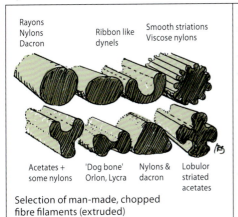

Rayons
Nylons
Dacron

Ribbon like dynels

Smooth striations
Viscose nylons

Acetates + some nylons

'Dog bone' Orlon, Lycra

Nylons & dacron

Lobulor striated acetates

Selection of man-made, chopped fibre filaments (extruded)

Solid, extruded filaments do not wick or absorb water. May stretch. Can be chopped any length. Smooth surface, uniform and consistent diameter, length and shape that can be regulated to a high degree. Melts at low temperatures then burns out in firing, leaving a void. Most burn out below 450°C (842°F). High risk of VOC (volatile organic carbon) vapour during firing. Inert, and resists water if combined with paperclay. Nano, thin versions of fibres are in development, for uses such as nano-mesh filtration.

Sources include: Petrochemicals derived from deposits of fuels, crude oil, natural gases, coal, etc.

Examples include: Nylon, rayon, acrylic, vinyl, polyester, polypropylene, fibrous forms of acetate, polymers, polyamide, polyolefins, polycarbonates, polystyrenes, hydrocarbons.

Synthetic ceramic fibres

Solid extruded ceramic filaments can be added to under-performing base clay to correct fired weakness where it is impractical to correct the root cause (base clay recipe). Can be added to paperclay for the same purpose. Ceramic fibre *remains in the clay body after firing* and does not melt or vapourise when used in a paperclay. Woven cloth of ceramic fibre can be dipped in paperclay and fired.

Source material includes: Fibrous inorganic substances, asbestos and aramids derived from composites of rock, clay, slag, or glass.

Examples include: Dry fluff form of fibreglass, kaowool, glass filaments, mineral wool (rockwool and slagwool), and specialty-use refractory ceramic fibers. Vitreous or porous ceramics for acoustic or thermal insulation fire-proofing, automotive, reinforced plastics and concrete, and as electrical insulation and plumbing material, ballistics, etc. Many of these highly-refined and pre-fired forms of ceramic materials in the form of refractory fibres have a high 'carbon footprint', so should be used responsibly.

9: Particle sizes: comparison of additions to clay bodies

Base clay ingredients vary greatly in particle size. In addition to the chemical make-up of ceramic ingredients, which is beyond the scope of this book, the size and amount of additive particles (grog, sand and filler) can be a factor in reducing the fired performance of your paperclay.

To convert a locally-dug clay to a paperclay and avoid dust, let the pebbles and large particles in a slip mixture settle to the bottom of the container overnight. Skim the smaller, lighter-weight particles off the top and middle to use for a base clay slip.

US Mesh Tyler scale (openings/sq. in. in sieve)	Metric 'mm' size (size of each opening in sieve)	Examples
1s mesh	26.5 mm	Gravel
2.5s mesh	8.0 mm	P-grog-chamotte (maximum)
3s mesh	6.7 mm	Sawdust – size varies
5s mesh	4.0 mm	Perlite (4s mesh, max.)
8s mesh	2.36 mm	Small cellulose fibres
20s mesh	850 μ	Coarse grog/chamotte
35s mesh	425 μ	Grogs/chamottes, large kyanite
42s mesh	355 μ	Fine grog or chamotte
65s mesh	212 μ	Very fine grain sand
200s mesh	75 μ	Glazes
325s mesh	45 μ	Glazes – small kyanites
400s mesh	36 μ	Small fireclay particle sizes
	10 μ – 0.2 μ	Average size range for clay particles: kaolins, ball and china clays
	1 μ = 0.001 mm	Small bacteria
	0.1 μ	Large colloidal particles – bentonites
	0.01 μ	Large molecule

Data for this chart and diagram in section 10 compiled by Rosette Gault from W. S. Tyler Inc. chart, Parmelee, Whitney, Cardew and Company, clay manufacturers.

10: Particle sizes: visual comparison

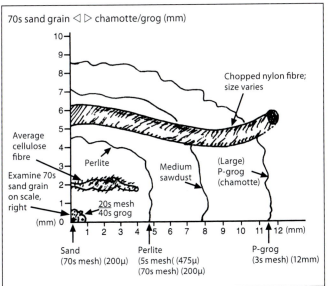

70s sand grain ◁ ▷ chamotte/grog (mm)

Chopped nylon fibre; size varies

Average cellulose fibre

Perlite

Medium sawdust

(Large) P-grog (chamotte)

Examine 70s sand grain on scale, right

20s mesh 40s grog

(mm)

Sand (70s mesh) (200μ)

Perlite (5s mesh((475μ) (70s mesh) (200μ)

P-grog (3s mesh) (12mm)

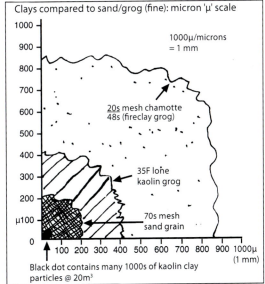

Clays compared to sand/grog (fine): micron 'μ' scale

1000μ/microns = 1 mm

20s mesh chamotte 48s (fireclay grog)

35F lone kaolin grog

70s mesh sand grain

μ100

(1 mm)

Black dot contains many 1000s of kaolin clay particles @ 20m³

11: Paperclay memory

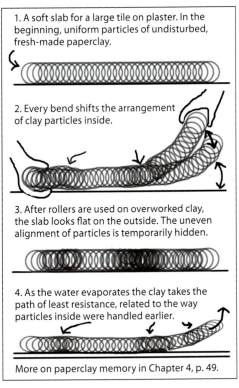

1. A soft slab for a large tile on plaster. In the beginning, uniform particles of undisturbed, fresh-made paperclay.

2. Every bend shifts the arrangement of clay particles inside.

3. After rollers are used on overworked clay, the slab looks flat on the outside. The uneven alignment of particles is temporarily hidden.

4. As the water evaporates the clay takes the path of least resistance, related to the way particles inside were handled earlier.

More on paperclay memory in Chapter 4, p. 49.

How warp occurs. *Illustration: Rosette Gault.*

12: Dry strength comparisons of base clay and paperclay

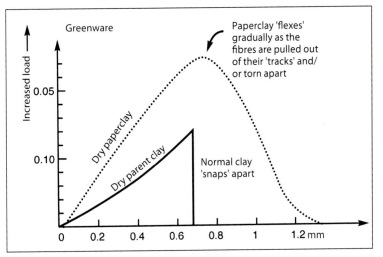

Greenware

Increased load →

Paperclay 'flexes' gradually as the fibres are pulled out of their 'tracks' and/ or torn apart

0.05

Dry paperclay

Dry parent clay

0.10

Normal clay 'snaps' apart

0   0.2   0.4   0.6   0.8   1   1.2 mm

Data compiled by author from Gault/Kingery Report, 1992.

13: Troubleshooting: avoid common mistakes

When pulp is not ready

If pulp is taking a long time to break down, you can:

1. Add more water. Pulp breaks apart much faster in plenty of water.

2. Use a different mixing tool – many are unsuitable.

3. Beat the pulp soup again, then gather or rub not-quite-ready wet pulp out of the water with a strainer, replace the water with hot water, put the pulp back in, and resume agitation. Multiple rubbings through a screen help break the pulp down further.

4. Did you mix different paper types in the same water? Mix pulp from each separately before combining. Gloss with matt, for instance, or black and white newsprint containing inserts, will cause lumps.

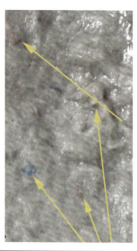

Over-squeezing wet pulp

Beware squeezing too much water out of wet pulp during straining. Doing this creates hard little wads or pebbles of pulp, shown below. These will not break apart in the slip and show up as air pockets or voids in the clay, before and after firing.

Problems with dry 'fluff' recycled pulp

Dry pulp mixes and insulation bagged from building suppliers is usually treated with flame retardants. During firing, smoke from paper burnout continues long past natural 2–3 hour time frame. These fumes are toxic. Flecks of paper like those seen here will show up as air pockets after fire.

Drying cracks due to low-pulp recipe

Hairline drying cracks like these can often be coated with a layer of higher pulp patch before fire.
After fire or bisque repair success rate of hairline crack repair is much lower than a patch over dry. Use more pulp in recipe next time to avoid this.

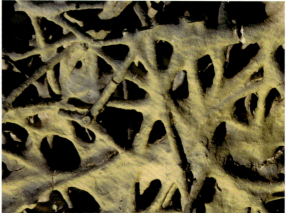

Pulp taking too long to break down

Though it is possible to stir small batches by hand, using a heavy-duty drill with a propeller-blade attachment saves time, especially if you are recycling paper on your own. Mixing tools that are designed for liquids are not recommended. Plenty of hot water to make a thin soup may lessen breakdown time. Papers vary, sort before pulping begins (pp. 146). Photo: Rosette Gault

Fired piece too fragile for handling

In this example, even though the thin, paperclay-coated stem wire seemed strong enough when dry, after firing the stem became the most vulnerable, brittle part, even with multiple coatings.

Plan ahead for life after the kiln. Create a shelter, frame or box (of paperclay if desired) to keep and transport delicate fired works safely. (Dry parts floral assembly in progress by Cory Olewnik (USA) Photo: Rosette Gault)

Microbial growth: aging

To remove visible surface growth off a moist lump of porcelain scrape with a rib. Moist paperclays vary widely in rate and types of microbe growth over time. Organic ingredients in the red or white base clays, pulps interact with water, air, and temperature so wide variety of microbes may spawn over time.

Those sensitive to microbial growth or mold should use fresh made to minimize risk of exposure and test small samples first.

Dried paperclay can be stored for many years with minimal growth. Prepare flat bread slices, tiles or patties to dry. Reclaim quickly next workperiod (see p. 144.) Photo: Rosette Gault

Deforming and melting in the kiln

Any clay will deform if fired to its melting point. Don't blame the paper, which fired out of the clay at about 253°C (451°F)! When your kiln is fired close to the maximum for the base clay, plan a support system, as explained in Chapter 8. Pay attention to placement in the kiln, as explained in Chapter 11.

The weight of a top-heavy form can overwhelm thin and unsupported walls located in the base of larger structures. Reinforce these complex forms wherever possible. Photo: Julia Nema

14: Shared properties: Mixed media vs. paperclay

- dry paperclay flexes and supports (like metal and wire)
- castable and carvable (like plaster and gypsum)
- castable and could be glazed for outdoors (like cement)
- carvable and durable (like stone)
- castable and mouldable can be a shell (like fibreglass)
- can be lightweight ceramic refractory and porous (like clay filters and/or bricks)
- can be durable and hard (like glazed ceramic)
- can be used on the wheel (like potter's clay)
- can be modelled (like oil-based modelling clay)
- high green tensile strength (like clay with man-made fibre)
- folds, cuts, casts, carves (like paper)
- can be modelled in open air and air hardens (like pâpier maché and doll-craft clay)

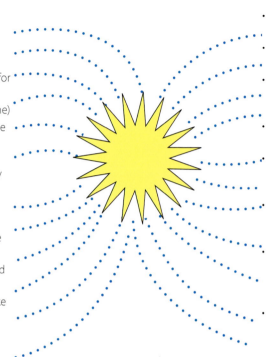

- flexes when dry (like poster and cardboard)
- folds and drapes when slabs are leathersoft (like canvas and fabric)
- at leathersoft can be braided, twisted, coiled, woven (like fabric)
- can be carved, cut and sawn when dry (like wood)
- hard and soft forms can be regulated and joined together (like modelling waxes)
- can soften and harden as it is modelled (like polymer modelling clays)
- can be used for press moulds and imprinting stamps and textures (like resins, hard and soft latex and rubbers)
- can be fluid, solid, pliant or flexing (like shrink wrap and other man-made plastics and materials).

Moulds

Paperclay ceramic can be used with sculptors' or injection moulds. More research is underway for crossover to bronze/lost-wax casting intermediate moulds. Most mixed media sculptors' release agents are compatible. Since paperclay shares many attributes with wax, sculptors are adapting it for this purpose also.

Printing and surface texture

The 3M product Cyrell® plate, used in industry for printing cardboard packaging, is compatible with paperclay. An image is produced by exposing a high-contrast print to the light-sensitive plate, which gives fine detail, and its rubbery texture makes it easy to press into paperclay lethersoft porcelain to get a bas relief print (contributed by Gaye Stevens, Australia).

Paperclay compared to papier-mâché and hobby modelling compounds:

Air-set paperclay weighs a little more than papier-mâché, which is composed of a majority paper pulp, glue and a trace of clay. The glue hardens the mix in the air. As paper burns at 233°C (451°F), these structures can turn to dust if fired in a kiln.

Modelling compounds that typically include plastics, perfumes, bright colours, acrylics, oils, wax, precious metals, polymers, etc, are too expensive for large-scale projects. Examples include the air-set hobby product Creative Paper Clay, by doll makers and jewellers, Sculpy®, Play Dough®, Celluclay® ,Silly Putty®, and others. A few of the polymer modelling compound products harden if heated in a kitchen oven but will melt into a puddle at high temperatures.

15: Paperclay vs. traditional clay practice

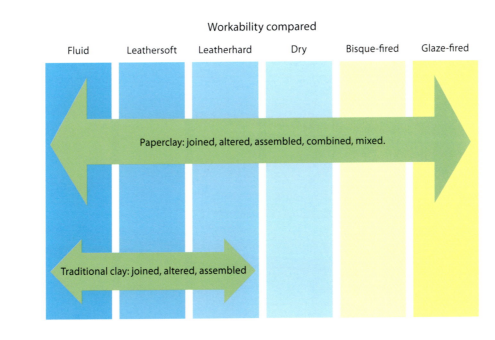

Workability compared

| Fluid | Leathersoft | Leatherhard | Dry | Bisque-fired | Glaze-fired |

Paperclay: joined, altered, assembled, combined, mixed.

Traditional clay: joined, altered, assembled

16: Design plan

Often this is an informal document, but in large-scale projects a design plan will give everyone a sense of what the project involves and what to expect. Factors to consider and include in the plan are:

- **The visual:** Model in scale and sketches
- **Brief summary:** Including date, time, place, participants
- **The site:** Interior/exterior, exposed to weather/people
- **Lighting:** Location, type, number and life span
- **Maintenance and care:** Finish needed, cleaning methods/frequency
- **Timeline:** Phases and milestones in the project and time for each
- **Measurements:** Limits such as size of kiln, doorways, transport vehicles. A scale model in advance will help.
- **Materials:** What is needed and when?
- **Handling and storage in studio:** Space needed for measuring a layout, assembly and storage

- **Packing, handling, shipping:** Requirements (e.g. size, source) for boxes or crates, packing materials, overseas shipping regulations, time needed
- **Transport:** Booking, size, human resources, extra equipment (e.g. forklift, truck, tools)
- **Installation:** Photos or videos for installation instructions may be helpful. Also consider tools and time needed for mounting.
- **Presentation and publicity:** Labelling, recording installation, press kit, promotional material, documentation
- **De-installation:** As above.
- **Lifespan:** Cost of replacement, estimates in time and materials
- **Insurance:** Who is responsible for loss, damage, or injury in connection with the work?
- **Budget:** Based on all factors considered above.

17: Further study

A full list of study resources is available on my website at www.paperclayart.com/191topics.html, but here is a selection of books, multimedia and articles that can serve as a starting point for learning more.

Artists and contributors in this book
See www.paperclayart.com/191ThankYou.html.

Selected books/media on paperclay
Gault, R 1998, 2008, *Paper Clay*, A & C Black, London; U. of Pennsylvania Pressm USA; Artisan Craft/Allen and Unwin, Australia; Gault, R 1993, 1994, 2003, 2006, 2010, *Paper clay for ceramic sculptors: A studio companion*, Clear Light Books/New Century Art Books, Seattle. Gault, R 1996, *At a Paperclay Workshop*, video demonstrations; Gault, R 2006, *Think By Hand: Hundreds of Possibilities for Paperclay Projects*; Kim, J 2006, *Paper-Composite Porcelain: Characterisation of Material Properties and Workability from a Ceramic Art and Design Perspective*, University of Gothenburg, Sweden; Lightwood, A 2008, *Paperclay and other clay additives*, Crowood Press, UK; Tardio-Brise, L 2008, *La terre-papier, Techniques et création*, Eyrolles, Paris.

Explore paperclay science and art
The following are a selection of journals and periodicals that contain articles involving ceramic paperclay: Artegia la Ceramica (Italy); Artists Newsletter (UK); Ceramic Review (UK); Ceramic: Art and Perception (Australia); Ceramics Monthly (USA); Ceramics Technical (USA/Australia); Keramik Magazin (Germany); La Revue du Ceramique et du Verre (France); New Ceramics (Germany); Revista Ceramica (Spain); The Journal of Australian Ceramics/ Pottery in Australia (Australia); 1280C Ceramic Art Magazine (Israel).

Paperclay research topics
Many authors have been contributing research on paperclay in recent years. Topics include: art studio practice and aesthetics, sustainable materials research, research and materials analysis of paperclay, porcelain paperclay and translucency, print and paperclay, paperclay curriculum and pedagogy, mixed media combined with paperclays, CAD/CAM computer modelling prototyping, and multimedia and cultural restoration. Find sources and research links listed at www.paperclayart.com/191topics.html

Sampling of exhibitions and events
Ceramic Arts and Design for a Sustainable Society, Gothenberg, Sweden (2011) (with symposium); Terre Papier, curated by Christelle Terrier, catalogue edited by Jean Luc Le Jeune, Musee Bernard Palissy, st. Avit, France (2011); Post-Modern Ceramics Exhibition at Varazdin Croatia curated by Bernd Pfannkuche (2009); Paperclay International Exhibit at Kesckemet, Hungary (2004, 2012) (with symposium); Paperclay Today at California, USA (2010) (with symposium), Seattle Tacoma International Airport Models for Waterfront Pier and Designs for Handheld Water Filtration (2012).

18: Suppliers

If you are not mixing paperclay from your own base clay, please consult www.paperclayart.com/120Suppliers.html for the most up-to-date links for suppliers of fresh-made high-performance ceramic paperclay (trademarked P'Clay® and P'Slip®, US. Pat. 5,726,111). These manufacturers can tell you where/who your nearest distributor is. Ready-to-use pug-milled paperclay can be rated for high-fire, low fire, or mid-range, for oxidation or reduction, wood, electric, gas, raku or pit firing, or just used as air-set. P'Clay® can be made from earthenware, terracotta (red clays), stoneware, porcelain, china clay and casting slip also.

Beware: Non-trademarked ready-blend paperclay from other suppliers is unlikely to reach the high performance standards taught in this book. It will have increased green strength, but is better to use with the traditional ceramic approach.

Commercial manufacturers can have their proprietary base clay recipes prepared as a reliable and consistent version of the author's trademarked P'Clay® and P'Slip® ceramic paperclays to meet expectation for the highest standards of quality, consistency, reliability and performance. Please contact the author via www.paperclayart.com to learn more benefits of being part of the network of licensees.

UK

Paperclay Products
Sharman Cottage, Howle Hill, Ross-on-Wye, Herefordshire, HR9 5ST
01989566672

Scarva Pottery Supplies Flaxclay
Unit 20, Scarva Road Industrial Estate,
Banbridge, Northern Ireland
BT32 3QD
028406-69699

TCAS (Metrosales)
Unit 3, 46 Mill Place
Kingston upon Thames
KT12 2RL
02085461108

USA

Aardvark Pottery Supply
www.aardvarkclay.com
Santa Ana, (714) 541-4157
Las Vegas, NV (702) 451-9898

Clay Art Center
www.clayartcenter.com
Tacoma, Washington
1-800-952-8030 (toll free)

East Bay Clay Custom Batch
Richmond, California
(San Francisco Bay Area)
510-233-1800

Industrial Minerals IMCO
www.clayimco.com
Sacramento, California
916-383-2811

Tuckers Pottery Supply
www.tuckerspottery.com
Richmond Hill, (Toronto) Canada
1-800-304-6185 (toll free)

19: Example recipes

Test-fire example recipes with your own materials first. I cannot be held responsible for non-standard materials, events and results that are beyond my control. On big projects, I always pre-test fire samples of each fresh made studio batch of pulp, baseclay/glaze/kiln to verify color, texture, weight, and finish. The author cannot guarantee that unlicensed non-trademark commercially made paperclay batches have the right amount of pulp to get the wet-dry join and other advantages. Always test fire before use. The recipes below can be used for large-scale outdoor/indoor sculpture. Most all paperclay recipes are easier to handle if bisquefired to cone 04, some degrees hotter than traditional bisque temperatures.

'Rosetta Stone' earthenware to mid-range paperclay for scupture (Cone 04–6)

This was my 'high-fire, low-fire', high-pulp, all-purpose, any kiln, any time sculpture clay for years.

Recipe:

- Two medium buckets of prepared earthenware-base, low-fire casting slip, rated cone 04–05
- One medium bucket of pulp, plus or minus a few handfuls (disperse paper from 8–12 rolls of bargain toilet tissue or 8 bulkier rolls of standard toilet tissue)
- Texture after fire: Smooth and white, the higher it is fired, the more dense and hard it gets after cone 4, even though the base clay is not rated that high.
- Cone 04–6: Hard as rock, resembles white stoneware. OK outdoors and in thaw, glazed or not glazed.

'Porcelain Pearl' paperclay for sculpture

Thin areas go translucent at cone 8. Fire to cone 10 only if walls are thick and other factors mentioned in this text indicate the structure is stable. For mixing batches in the studio, avoid airborne dust clouds by starting with buckets of prepared liquid casting/pouring slip rather than bags of powdered clay.

Recipe:

- Two medium buckets of prepared 'porcelain' (cone 10) high-fire casting slip

- One medium bucket of pulp plus or minus a few handfuls (disperse paper from 8–12 rolls of bargain toilet tissue or 8 bulkier rolls of standard toilet tissue)
- High fire: Cone 8–10 hard as rock. If walls are thin, go to cone 8 and play it safe to avoid deformation. Do not maintain the kiln at high temperature or extended reduction as this will increase risk of hot spot deformation. Load kilns evenly. Serious power tools needed to alter surface.

Substitutions and adaptations for Rosette recipes

High-fire stoneware as base clay:

If you substitute stoneware throwing clay as the base for a porcelain base clay (Porcelain Pearl), the stoneware version fires tan to brown.

Addition of perlite:

Paperclays with added perlite ("Ruff-Rock-Gruff-Rock"), fire very lightweight and hard like stone at high temperatures. They can be carved with hammer and chisel (see p. 69). Because non-clay perlite (like grog/chamotte) does not shrink, if you add too much, it tends to crack when fired. Add equal parts of clay to match the amount of perlite you add. Test first to fine-tune the recipe to your own needs.

For large-scale sculpture (Wali Hawes, India):

Three recipes that work really well for large-scale paperclay work. Note how much variation there can be.
- Recipe CB4: 1 part paper pulp, 4 parts refractory clay, 3 parts talc, ½ part wollastonite, ½ part alumina, ½ part grog/firebrick.
- Recipe CB5: 2 parts paper pulp, 3 parts refractory clay, 1 part grog/firebrick, ¼ part wollastonite, ½ part alumina.
- Recipe CB6: 1 part paper pulp, 2 parts refractory clay, 1 part terracotta, 1 part grog/firebrick, ¼ part wollastonite.

Eszter Imre (Sweden), *We will cross that bridge when we get there*, 2011. Porcelain paperclay casting, 33 x 32 x 15 cm (13 x 12½ x 6 in.). *Photo: Johannes Holberg.*

Studio recipe shortcuts (Trudy Golley, Canada):

- This is Jen Clark's method of wedging pulp into pug-milled traditional clay without making slip from it first. Place a single layer of two-ply toilet paper directly onto the slab slice(s) of traditional moist clay. With a spray bottle, moisten the paper gently so it will not soak moisture from the clay below and wedge the damp wet tissue layer in.
- Working with fibre in my clay triggered an investigation into using fibre in plaster to make thin strong moulds. Find articles Golley has written about these techniques in *Ceramics Technical*.

Paperclay casting slip:

These methods are contributed by multiple artists, all using traditional linear methods.

- Add paper pulp in small amounts (1–5% by volume) to casting slip. "I found that over time I desired, and required, less and less paper fibre in my clay. I wanted the fibre to give the reinforcing qualities without getting in the way. I started with 25% fibre and have now reduced the amount to ½–1% by volume."
- From Sandra Black (Australia): "Trudy Golley introduced me to putting a small amount of toilet paper, around 1 teaspoon per litre, into my slip. It stopped all the rim splitting I used to have in my slip castings."

Burnout additives in porcelain and/or bone china paperclay slip recipes (Luca Tripaldi, Italy):

To get rich textures and colours embedded in the paperclay after fire, match the volume of cellulose to the volume of solid intentional materials added to liquid porcelain paperclay slip. These could be ceramic colour-stained porcelain bisque ground into small chunks, ground up cork pieces, bits of preroasted dried seed, wood, pine needles, straw sliced into needles, etc. If I go beyond 30% of solid material pieces in a high-pulp paperclay slip, the clay will be too short to work with.

I go very slowly, firing thick-walled bowls to 315°C (600°F) in a 6-hour bisque firing. I rinse with water, cleaning up residual ash, and wet-polish by sanding wth wet and dry sandpaper, 400 grit. When I have round-bottom bowls, I fire my pieces on a quartz sand temporary 'nest' on the kiln shelf. The base clay recipe I use for porcelain is bone ash 30, china clay 30, ball clay 20, nepheline 20 (by weight).

Index